Framing Film Festivals

Series Editors
Marijke de Valck, Department of Media and Culture Studies, Utrecht University, Utrecht, The Netherlands
Tamara L. Falicov, Dean, School of Humanities and Social Sciences, Department of Media, Art, and Design, University of Missouri-Kansas City, Kansas City, MO, USA

Every day, somewhere in the world a film festival takes place. Most people know about the festival in Cannes, the world's leading film festival, and many will also be familiar with other high profile events, like Venice, the oldest festival; Sundance, America's vibrant independent scene; and Toronto, a premier market place. In the past decade the study of film festivals has blossomed. A growing number of scholars recognize the significance of film festivals for understanding cinema's production, distribution, reception and aesthetics, and their work has amounted to a prolific new field in the study of film culture. The Framing Film Festivals series presents the best of contemporary film festival research. Books in the series are academically rigorous, socially relevant, contain critical discourse on festivals, and are intellectually original. Framing Film Festivals offers a dedicated space for academic knowledge dissemination.

Sheila Petty
Editor

African Film Festivals and Transnational Flows of Living Cultural Heritage

palgrave
macmillan

Editor
Sheila Petty
Department of Film
University of Regina
Regina, SK, Canada

ISSN 2946-3734 ISSN 2946-3742 (electronic)
Framing Film Festivals
ISBN 978-3-031-88589-1 ISBN 978-3-031-88590-7 (eBook)
https://doi.org/10.1007/978-3-031-88590-7

© The Editor(s) (if applicable) and The Author(s) 2025. This book is an open access publication.

Open Access This book is licensed under the terms of the Creative Commons Attribution 4.0 International License (http://creativecommons.org/licenses/by/4.0/), which permits use, sharing, adaptation, distribution and reproduction in any medium or format, as long as you give appropriate credit to the original author(s) and the source, provide a link to the Creative Commons license and indicate if changes were made.
The images or other third party material in this book are included in the book's Creative Commons license, unless indicated otherwise in a credit line to the material. If material is not included in the book's Creative Commons license and your intended use is not permitted by statutory regulation or exceeds the permitted use, you will need to obtain permission directly from the copyright holder.
The use of general descriptive names, registered names, trademarks, service marks, etc. in this publication does not imply, even in the absence of a specific statement, that such names are exempt from the relevant protective laws and regulations and therefore free for general use.
The publisher, the authors and the editors are safe to assume that the advice and information in this book are believed to be true and accurate at the date of publication. Neither the publisher nor the authors or the editors give a warranty, expressed or implied, with respect to the material contained herein or for any errors or omissions that may have been made. The publisher remains neutral with regard to jurisdictional claims in published maps and institutional affiliations.

Cover credit: @ Estrella Sendra

This Palgrave Macmillan imprint is published by the registered company Springer Nature Switzerland AG
The registered company address is: Gewerbestrasse 11, 6330 Cham, Switzerland

If disposing of this product, please recycle the paper.

Acknowledgments

This book would not have been possible without the generous support of several people and organizations.

Thanks are due to all the contributors for their interesting and innovative chapters, without which this book could never have come to fruition.

I would like to express my deep and sincere gratitude to my friend and colleague Dr. Estrella Sendra for designing such an original and creative book cover.

I am also very thankful to my research assistant, Fausto Llampallas Iturriría, for photography assistance, and to Barb Flynn and Bob Gilongos at the University of Regina for ongoing research and project management advice.

The research for this book was supported, in part, by the Social Sciences and Humanities Research Council of Canada Partnership Development Grant #890-2020-0102 and, in part, by the Government of Canada's New Frontiers in Research Fund for the project, *Decolonizing Film Festival Research in a Post-Pandemic World* [NFRFR-2021-00161].

I gratefully acknowledge the support of the Social Sciences and Humanities Research Council of Canada Partnership Development Grant #890-2020-0102 that allowed this book to be published open access.

At Palgrave Macmillan and Springer Nature, I would like to thank all the editors, managers, and staff for their meticulous work, as well as the anonymous readers of the manuscript.

Finally, I thank Vaughn Borden, who gives me, as always, unconditional support.

PRAISE FOR *AFRICAN FILM FESTIVALS AND TRANSNATIONAL FLOWS OF LIVING CULTURAL HERITAGE*

"Sure to become a key reference for anyone working on, or in, African film festivals, this edited collection offers a refreshingly pluri-centric perspective on the ways African stories travel across many continents. Petty has brought together an inspiring array of academics and curators to offer much-needed insights into the mythologies, collaborations and communities that constitute today's African film worlds."

—Dr. Rachel Johnson, *University of Leeds, United Kingdom*

"This volume is an essential festival knowledge forum, centering culture and knowledge originating from the African continent. Through a diverse set of case studies on Africa-themed film festivals across Africa, the Americas, and Europe, it provides rich, collaborative insights from researchers, curators, and communities. The book offers highly engaging Indigenous, postcolonial, and diasporic perspectives, emphasizing the social impact, cultural exchange, and meaningful collaboration of and through film festivals."

—Prof. Dr. Skadi Loist, *Film University Babelsberg KONRAD WOLF, Germany*

"This edited collection provides a nuanced overview of the role played by international film festivals in shaping our understanding of African cinemas across the globe. Petty brilliantly brings together a wide range of scholars and critics to examine the communities and circuits through which African films circulate. A much-needed intervention in festival studies."

—Dr. Antoine Damiens, *York University, Canada*

Contents

1 Introduction: African Film Festivals and Transnational Flows of Living Cultural Heritage 1
Sheila Petty

2 On FESPACO Mythology 13
Olivier Barlet

3 Curating Africa in Contemporary Film Festivals in Senegal: An Analysis of the Constellation of Collaborations 35
Laura Feal and Estrella Sendra

4 Journeys of Discovery: The Case of the New York Forum of Amazigh Film (NYFAF) 57
Lucy R. McNair and Habiba Boumlik

5 Virtualization of the New York Forum of Amazigh Film (NYFAF) During and Post-COVID-19: The Scramble "To Remain the Same" 79
Soubeika Bahri

6 From Africa to London to the World: Film Africa's Leading Role in the Circulation of African Cinemas 101
Estrella Sendra and Robin Steedman

7 African Film Festivals: A Transnational Programming Intervention and *Tales of the Accidental City* as a Case Study   123
Giovana Nabarrete de Souza Cruz and Babatunde Onikoyi

8 "Act in Your Location, Think with the World": Constructing Audience "Afterlives" at Three North American-Based African Film Festivals   141
Sheila Petty and Estrella Sendra

Index   161

Notes on Contributors

Soubeika Bahri holds a PhD in Linguistics and M.A. in Applied Linguistics. Her research examines language maintenance and revitalization of the Tunisian variety of Tamazight, both at the structural level and through the computer-mediated discourse. Her recent work has turned to diverse topics that include language and cinematic discourse in Amazigh film and language and gender inclusivity in writing Arabic varieties. Dr. Bahri is co-editor of the volume *Digital Orality: Vernacular Writing in the Online Spaces*. Currently, she serves as an associate editor of the *Journal of Amazigh Studies* and a co-organizer of the New York Forum of Amazigh Film.

Olivier Barlet was born in Paris in 1952. He has translated a number of books on Africa and was literary agent specialized on Africa. He is a member of the Syndicat français de la critique de cinéma, and is Cinema Editorial Director for *Africultures*, after having been a long-time film correspondent for Africa International, Afrique-Asie and Continental. His books have been translated into English: *African Cinemas, Decolonizing the Gaze* (Zed Books, London, 1997), and *Contemporary African Cinema* (Michigan State University Press, 2016). He has written 1800 articles on African film for the *Africultures* and *Afrimages* websites.

Habiba Boumlik is a professor at LaGuardia Community College, CUNY, specializing in Arabic, French, and Middle Eastern cinema. She founded the New York Forum of Amazigh Film, promoting Amazigh/

Berber culture. Her notable publications include *"Indigeneity and Identity Transmission: Amazigh Cultural Expression through Film"* (2023) and *"Morocco's Islamic Feminism"* (2018). Dr. Boumlik's research focuses on cultural identity, social change, and historical memory, contributing significantly to the understanding of North African societies and their diaspora.

Laura Feal is a PhD candidate at Université Gaston Berger (Saint-Louis) whose work focuses on memories of cinemagoing in the twentieth century in Saint-Louis. She is a journalist, independent researcher, and project manager with expertise in international cooperation, working in various African countries such as Algeria, Morocco, Namibia, Mozambique, and Mauritania. Based in Senegal since 2012, she is involved in several community-based cultural initiatives, coordinating the activities of the local association Hahatay. Since 2018, she has been a regular contributor to the Spanish newspaper *EL PAÍSA* and other media. She is a member of the artistic committee of the international documentary film festival, StLouis'DOCS.

Lucy R. McNair is a translator and professor of English at LaGuardia Community College, The City University of New York, where she teaches writing and literature, co-leads a faculty seminar on Language Across the Curriculum, and co-curates the New York Forum of Amazigh Film (www.nyfaf.com). Translator of Mouloud Feraoun's Algerian-Amazigh classic, *The Poor Man's Son*, her scholarly articles have appeared in *Jadaliyya*, *Language, Culture and Curriculum*, and *Journal of North African Studies*. With Yahya Laayouni, she is co-editor of the collection, *Amazigh Cinema: An Introduction to North African Indigenous Film* (University of Regina Press, 2025).

Babatunde Onikoyi is a PhD candidate and sessional lecturer in the Department of Film, University of Regina, Canada. He is also film reviews editor for *African Studies Review*. His essays on African cinemas have appeared in prestigious journals and book volumes, including *Black Camera*, *Journal of African Literature Association*, *African Studies Review*, *Africa Studies Quarterly,* and *Journal of African Cinemas,* among others. His research interests include Transnational Screen Media, Film Festivals, Cultural and Diaspora Studies, and Global Cinemas. He is the co-editor of *The Cinema of Tunde Kelani: Aesthetics, Theatricalities and Visual Performance* (Cambridge Scholars, 2021).

Sheila Petty is a Fellow of the Royal Society of Canada and Professor Emerita of Film Studies at the University of Regina, Canada. She held the SaskPower Research Chair in Cultural Heritage at the University of Regina from 2022 to 2024. She has written extensively on manifestations of cultural heritage in sub-Saharan African, North African, and Amazigh cinemas and has curated exhibitions for art galleries across Canada. Her latest project, funded through the Government of Canada's New Frontiers in Research Fund, investigates methodologies for decolonizing film festival research in a post-pandemic world. Her most recent book is *Habiba Djahnine: Memory Bearer* (Edinburgh University Press, 2025).

Estrella Sendra is Lecturer in Culture, Media and Creative Industries Education (Festivals and Events) at King's College London. Her main research interests are film and creative industries in Senegal, with a particular focus on festivals. She was the co-principal investigator of "Decolonizing Film Festival Research in a Post-Pandemic World," funded by the Government of Canada's New Frontiers in Research Fund (NFRFR-2021-00161, 2022–24). She is an advisory board member of the ERC-funded research project "African Screen Worlds: Decolonising Film and Screen Studies" (grant agreement No. 819236, 2019–24), led by Prof. Lindiwe Dovey. In 2024, she was awarded the King's Research Impact Awards (International Collaboration) for her collaborations with festivals and film programs curating African cinemas.

Giovana Nabarrete de Souza Cruz holds a Bachelor's in Film Production degree through the University of Regina. She has been involved in Dr. Petty's film festival research since 2022, for which she devised a programming intervention and wrote a festival review. Her research interests are transnational cinema, exoticism in cinematic representations, and the crossing of philosophical theories and filmmaking. Beyond working as a filmmaker and academic, Giovana is also an analogue film photographer and the manager of in-competition programming for the Regina International Film Festival and Awards.

Robin Steedman is Lecturer in creative industries at the University of Glasgow. She is interested in African creative and cultural industries and in questions of diversity and inequality in media production, distribution, and viewership. Her work on African creative industries has been published in journals such as *Poetics, Information, Communication and Society, Cultural Trends, Environment and Planning A, Geoforum,* and

International Journal of Cultural Studies. Her first book is *Creative Hustling: Women Making and Distributing Films from Nairobi* (MIT Press).

Acronyms and Abbreviations

ACM	Amazigh Cultural Movement (CMA Congrès Mondial Amazigh)
ALA	Congreso Latinoamericano de Antropología
AM-FM	African Movie Festival in Manitoba
AMREC	Association Marocaine de Recherches et d'Echanges Culturels
ASCC	Association Sénégalaise de la Critique Cinématographique (Senegalese Association of Film Critics)
BFI	British Film Institute
CCM	Moroccan Cinematographic Center (CCM)
CIFF	Cairo International Film Festival
CIFF	Cleveland International Film Festival
Cinefemfest	Festival africain du film et de la recherche féministes
CUNY	City University of New York
DIFF	Durban International Film Festival
DocAnt	National Showcase of Anthropological and Social Documentary Film and Video
FACC	Fédération africaine de la critique cinématographique/African Federation of Film Critics
FCNFA	Festival Culturel National du Film Amazigh
FEPACI	Fédération Panafricaine des Cinéastes
FESPACO	Festival panafricain du cinéma et de la télévision de Ouagadougou (Panafrican Film and Television Festival of Ouagadougou)
FFA	Film Festival Alliance
FFFA	Festival Films Femmes Afrique
FFM	Festival Films Femmes Méditerranée in Marseille

FIAPF	Fédération internationale des associations de producteurs de films/International Federation of Film Producers Associations
FIFF	Festival International de Films de Femmes (Cotonou, Benin)
FIFFS	Festival International du Film de Femmes de Salé (Morocco)
FINIFA	Issni N'Ourgh (International Festival of Amazigh Film in Agadir)
FIPRESCI	Fédération internationale de la presse cinématographique/International Federation of Film Critics
FOPICA	Funds for the Promotion of the Cinematographic and Audiovisual Industry
IACHR	Inter-American Commission on Human Rights
INAFEC	Institut Africain d'Education Cinématographique
INAPL	National Institute of Anthropology and Latin American Thought
JCC	Journées cinématographiques de Carthage
JCFA	Journées cinématographiques de la femme africaine de l'image
JIFA	Les Journées Internationales du Film Amazigh
LIFF	Leeds International Film Festival
LPAC	LaGuardia Performing Arts Center
LSSFF	Living Skies Student Film Festival
MOSTRA	Mostra de Cinemas Africanos
NYFAF	New York Forum of Amazigh Film
ONF/NFB	Office national du film du Canada/National Film Board of Canada
RAM	Reunión de Antropología del Mercosur
RAS	Royal African Society
RECIDAK	Les Rencontres cinématographiques internationales de Dakar
RED	Red de Festivales y Muestras de Cine de Chile y los Pueblos Originarios (Network of Chilean and Indigenous Film Festivals
REMAV	Red Mexicana de Antropologia Visual
RIFFA	Regina International Film Festival and Awards
SDLFF	San Diego Latino Film Festival
SIFF	Seattle International Film Festival
SOAS	School of Oriental and African Studies, University of London
StLouis'Docs	Festival International du Film Documentaire de Saint-Louis
SXSW	South by Southwest
UNDRIP	United Nations Declaration on the Rights of Indigenous Peoples
VUES	Festival International de Cinéma Vues d'Afrique

List of Figures

Cover image "Drawing inspired by a pop-up screening at Ndiébène Gandiol, Senegal, during Festival StLouis'DOCS 2023" (Courtesy Estrella Sendra)

Chapter 2

Fig. 1 FESPACO 2023 official poster (Courtesy FESPACO. CC BY-SA 4.0.) — 14

Chapter 3

Fig. 1 Visualization of the constellation of entangled collaborations in the Festival Films Femmes Afrique (FFFA) in 2022 (Courtesy Laura Feal and Estrella Sendra 2021) — 47

Fig. 2 Visualization of the constellation of entangled collaborations in the Festival StLouis'DOCS in 2022 and 2023 (Courtesy Laura Feal and Estrella Sendra 2021) — 48

Chapter 4

Fig. 1 Poster for the 2017 3rd edition of New York Forum of Amazigh Film (NYFAF) (Courtesy New York Forum of Amazigh Film) — 64

Fig. 2	Poster for the 2019 5th edition of New York Forum of Amazigh Film (NYFAF) (Courtesy New York Forum of Amazigh Film)	68
Fig. 3	Poster for the 2023 8th edition of New York Forum of Amazigh Film (NYFAF) (Courtesy New York Forum of Amazigh Film)	70

Chapter 6

Fig. 1	Map showing the various locations Film Africa has been hosted over the years (*Source* Map elaborated by Estrella Sendra and Robin Steedman for the purpose of this chapter (2024). Courtesy Estrella Sendra and Robin Steedman). [The map can be accessed also via this link: https://maps.app.goo.gl/4UZBk1PsSW6si37W9] CC BY-SA 4	113
Fig. 2	Film Africa audiences gathering at the front entrance of Hackney Picturehouse in 2012 (Courtesy Estrella Sendra)	115

Chapter 7

Fig. 1	Poster for *Tales of the Accidental City* with insert photo of Maïmouna Jallow (Courtesy Maïmouna Jallow)	132

Chapter 8

Fig. 1	Poster for "Vues d'Afrique—40 Ans d'Affiches" exhibition at Maison du Conseil des Arts de Montréal during the Rallye-Expos 2024 (Courtesy Vues d'Afrique)	147
Fig. 2	2024 Poster for African Movie Festival in Manitoba (Courtesy African Movie Festival in Manitoba)	150
Fig. 3	IV Festival Artístico Audiovisual Afrodescendencias 2024 festival poster (Courtesy Claudia Lora)	154
Fig. 4	Pop-up screening of *Diablos, El Quizá Nueva Generación* (Claudia Lora, 2024, Mexico) at El Quizá, Guerrero on 7 June 2024 (Courtesy Rodrigo Martínez Vargas)	156

CHAPTER 1

Introduction: African Film Festivals and Transnational Flows of Living Cultural Heritage

Sheila Petty

Abstract Through case studies of African film festivals around the world, this book explores festivals as spaces of living cultural heritage involving multiple audiences that engage with local and transnational levels of meaning. The chapters probe how flows of knowledge that arise from the African continent arrive at African-themed film festivals (both on and off the continent) and are transformed through new contexts of presentation and engagement in new locations. The chapters examine how histories and memory are contextualized and translated across geographies and historiographies. The chapters investigate potential methods of catalyzing a "transnational flow" from inception to end that involves attention to process rather than studying festivals as static cultural products with discrete and isolated categories of programming, presentation, documentation, and networking. The chapters in this book advance understanding

S. Petty (✉)
Department of Film, University of Regina, Regina, SK, Canada
e-mail: Sheila.Petty@uregina.ca

© The Author(s) 2025
S. Petty (ed.), *African Film Festivals and Transnational Flows of Living Cultural Heritage*, Framing Film Festivals,
https://doi.org/10.1007/978-3-031-88590-7_1

of culturally situated views of systems and heritage as a human and transglobal preoccupation that must cross borders.

Keywords Africa · Film · Festival · Travel · Audience · Transnational · Cultural heritage

The human right to tell one's story in one's own language (cultural sovereignty), as embodied in the United Nations Declaration on the Rights of Indigenous Peoples (UNDRIP), is a crucial focus of recent scholarly research. Furthermore, global mobility has led scholars to ponder the nature of traveling ideas and theories. Theorists of globalization such as the Martinican Édouard Glissant (2009) and the Moroccan Abdelkébir Khatibi (1983) have cautioned that local histories are also the products of global interactions, including colonialism. Moroccan Amazigh writer and linguist Ahmed Boukouss reminds us that the Maghreb has always been a region of contact zones where diverse peoples, languages, and cultures from Punic, Greek, and Latin to Arabic, French, and Spanish have peacefully co-existed and even thrived through contact (2012, 69). Quite naturally, these transnational influences find their way into cultural production, regardless of the chosen form or mode. Cognizant of these current debates, this book aims to understand and communicate how cultural expressions travel, for example, from continental Africa and arrive in North America and Europe, and how they are articulated from the diaspora by many filmmakers in films which circulate back to the "homeland" and out again to multiple points of view. Respect for living cultural heritage as a manifest expression that transcends nations is imperative in a time of growing globalization, traveling, and travel bans due to pandemics, and the concomitant use of digital media to share living cultural expression, such as in curated spaces like film festivals.

Around the globe, film festivals offer platforms for understanding film cultures and their contexts of production, distribution and reception. From the world's first international film festival in Venice, Italy, in 1932, to more recently formed, identity-based local events, film festivals create spaces for dialogue and set the stage for audience engagement with moving image texts (Chan 2011). Beyond their exhibition and display function, festivals have often traditionally been considered catalysts for industry-oriented activity, such as financing, training, and networking. In the case of "Francophone Oceania," it is these very factors, according to Michelle Royer, that have prompted the establishment of film festivals in "New Caledonia, French Polynesia, and Wallis and Futuna" where Western media continue to dominate the audiovisual sector (2024, 66–67).

As African nations gained independence during the 1960s, festivals provided a mechanism to bring together filmmakers from around the continent keen to build viable film industries and contribute to their new nations' economic and cultural well-being. According to Lindiwe Dovey, "arts festivals with a strong film presence" took root "during decolonization," and by the mid-1960s "regularly held film festivals" emerged, such as the Journées cinématographiques de Carthage founded in Tunisia in 1966 and the Festival Panafricain du Cinéma et de la Télévision de Ouagadougou (FESPACO) in Burkina Faso (Dovey 2015, 1). These festivals aligned with the precepts laid out in the Algiers Charter on African Cinema, adopted at the Second Congress of the FEPACI (Fédération Panafricain des Cinéastes) in Algiers, in January 1975. Among other things, the Charter focused on the necessity of training future generations of filmmakers and capitalizing on Panafrican and transnational networking. It described cinema as a "stimulus to creativity," whereby the outcomes of expression were meant to be myriad, fluid, reconfigured, and remediated into multiple journeys, taking African cultures into the future. This underscores the thinking of Cameroonian philosopher Achille Mbembe, who has held that the "movement of worlds" as he describes it, creates histories that must be understood as "cultures of mobility" emerging in response to internal and external contacts (2002).

Many film festivals today take place within "contemporary transnational context(s) of exchange and production" (Boumlik and McNair 2017). Such is the case of four North American film festivals whose mandates include providing a meeting place and space of celebration and dialogue between diverse local communities and African cultures in globalizing contexts. Festival International de Cinéma Vues d'Afrique is North America's largest and longest-running African film festival. Established in Montreal in 1985 to introduce African and Creole cinema and culture to Quebec and Canada and to forge links with other African cinema festivals around the world (such as the Panafrican Film Festival of Ouagadougou and the Carthage Film Festival), the organizers have sought, over the years, to expand offerings for spectators beyond conventional categories of film production and exhibition. In 2015, Drs. Habiba

Boumlik and Lucy McNair established the first edition of the New York Forum of Amazigh Film with the goal of disseminating and encouraging Amazigh cinema and celebrating "the history, culture, and language of Amazigh peoples across North Africa and in the diaspora" (Boumlik and McNair 2017). The African Movie Festival in Manitoba (AM-FM) was founded in 2017 by Dr. Ben Akoh in Winnipeg, Manitoba, with the mandate to showcase the best of African Cinema and create a platform for Afro-Canadian dialogue. In Mexico, the Festival Artistico Audiovisual Afrodescendencias was founded in 2021 by a group of researchers, artists, activists, and communities to celebrate Afro-Mexican identity through a multidisciplinary and itinerant showcase of Afro-Mexican arts. These festivals, as well as others around the globe, that are discussed in this book, including Mostra de Cinemas Africanos in Brazil; Festival Films Femmes Afrique and StLouis'DOCS in Senegal; Leeds International Film Festival and Film Africa in the United Kingdom, all draw their knowledge foundation from within the Algiers Charter, embracing its pedagogical and creative directives, and creating spaces for cultural heritage to live, flourish, and evolve. The authors who have contributed to this book understand and consider festivals as spaces of living cultural heritage involving multiple audiences that engage with local and transnational levels of meaning.

The chapters position Africa as point of origin, thus challenging perceptions of the continent as "defined by a state of crisis," spurred on by failing economies and the ravages of war (Gikandi 630). The book disputes the view of Africa as "an object apart from the world," a view which "perpetually underplays the embeddedness in multiple elsewheres of which the continent actually speaks" (Mbembe and Nuttall 348). Rather, the book answers Achille Mbembe's call for the development of "an aesthetic of opening and encounter," whereby identities are intrinsically global in scope because they have been shaped by a confluence of transnational forces (2002, 640).

The chapters probe how flows of knowledge that arise from the African continent arrive at African-themed film festivals (both on and off the continent) and are realized/transformed through new contexts of presentation and engagement in new locations. We ask how histories and memory are contextualized and translated across geographies and historiographies. The chapters investigate potential methods of catalyzing a "transnational flow" from inception to end that involves attention to process rather than studying festivals as static cultural products with discrete and isolated categories of programming, presentation, documentation, and networking. The chapters also seek to understand several interrelated questions: how does a festival interact with place/location in using the city/location as its exhibition venue? How does a festival create a "journey of discovery" in translating and contextualizing films for specific populations and audiences and creating virtual and on-site dialogues? In engaging with audiences in the moment of viewing a film, how do we arrive at festivals and move along their circuits? What are the ethnographic methods, such as "being there" versus digital ethnography (Facebook, etc.), which allow one to witness certain events live, enabling audiences to move along the circuit when one cannot move along live? What is "giving back" (results sharing), and how is all of this multidirectional? What are the layers that safeguarding and archiving entail? How do archives curate their own stories about festivals?

This book extends activities funded through the Social Sciences and Humanities Research Council of Canada and awarded to Principal Investigator Sheila Petty to host a virtual conference, "Transnational Screen Media Practices: Safeguarding Cultural Heritage," at the University of Regina in June 2021 and a hybrid conference, "Film Festivals and Transnational Flows of Living Cultural Heritage: Africa in the World" in April 2023 during the Vues d'Afrique film festival in Montreal, and chapter contributors were participants in the events.

Through our approach of bridging cultural practices that constitute unique local heritages with transnational sites of cultural production through the medium of film, the chapter contributions to this book will advance understanding of cultural heritage as a human and transglobal preoccupation that must cross borders. This allows for a transnational, relational nexus between Africa and global influences—culturally situated views of systems and heritage—"living" embedded within epistemologies. Édouard Glissant's theory of "tout-monde" presents a starting point because it visualizes culture and art production as an unfolding process, subject to both internal and external cultural contacts where the "synthesis/genesis" of identity and aesthetics are continually evolving. The theory of "tout-monde" is grounded in the philosophy that the world is globalized, métissé, and creolized (adding a layer of unpredictability). Glissant would often repeat, "Agis dans ton lieu, pense avec le monde"/ act in your location, think with the world (2009, 87). Tout-mondism foregrounds a decentering of hegemonic and Eurocentric points of view and promotes interdisciplinarity. It also cautions that while "seeing and thinking large" (Imorou 2011, 34) it is important to take into consideration how the colonial past has informed present conditions of being. Chadwick Allen writes that "the local launches into the regional, national, or global only to become local again and again" evoking movement, flows, and journeys that are not linear but are "trans-yes, in the sense of across, beyond, and through, but not limited to national borders" (2012, 2).

In his chapter "On FESPACO Mythology," Olivier Barlet focuses on the Ouagadougou Pan-African Film and Television Festival (FESPACO) to probe how a myth is an imaginary construction that is the foundation of a social practice based on the values of a community seeking its cohesion. Since 1972, FESPACO has awarded the grand prize of the Stallion of Yennenga, in reference to a Mossi myth. The poster for the 2023 edition takes up the myth of this warrior woman who is also a builder of peace. FESPACO has always been like African cinema: a structuring myth. In 2023, a bust of Ousmane Sembène—himself a myth: "the father of African cinema"—was installed at the entrance to the FESPACO headquarters. But is the festival still aligned with the militant objectives defined by the great filmmaker? Whether it is a group of filmmakers or films, these fundamental issues have never ceased to be called into question. The rituals remain unchanged, as does the adjective "pan-African" in the festival's title. What kind of pan-Africanism are we talking about? This mythical notion itself evolves like cinema, around the question of African identity. Meanwhile, the festival continues to defend its centrality … because FESPACO is also a bastion. According to the Larousse French dictionary, a myth is a story, an allegory, a character, or a belief that expresses an idea or force. Barlet examines the Ouagadougou Pan-African Film and Television Festival (FESPACO) through this lens to consider how necessary this appeal to the imaginary was, and remains, for the African film festival to conserve its top spot.

In Chapter 3, "Curating Africa in Contemporary Film Festivals in Senegal: An Analysis of the Constellation of Collaborations," Laura Feal and Estrella Sendra examine how, seventy years after the first African-directed productions on the continent, the industry is still precarious and thus, some festivals in Senegal are innovatively networking and collaborating to build capacity and boost film circulation of both Senegalese and African films more broadly. This is a form of sustainability—a survival tactic—that involves sharing. It can best be described as a constellation of collaborations. The authors question the role of such collaborations in the representation and circulation of certain forms of African living cultural heritage and suggest that film festivals in Senegal operate as entangled constellations that forge a star system involving not just actors but also filmmakers and further agents involved in film production and circulation. These foster a transnational flow of films and film professionals, which operates as a "passport" for international exhibition platforms, thereby legitimizing the artistic value of these productions. The authors analyze two illustrative examples of festivals in Senegal that work in this direction, namely the Festival Films Femmes Afrique and the Festival StLouis' DOCS and seek to contribute to discussions on the curation of screen worlds and the shift from competition to collaboration in festivals and the cultural industries.

In Chapter 4, "Journeys of Discovery: The Case of the New York Forum of Amazigh Film (NYFAF)," Lucy R. McNair and Habiba Boumlik offer an in-depth analysis of the New York Forum of Amazigh Film (NYFAF), founded in 2015 and co-curated by the authors. They contend that culturally focused film festivals, though rooted in local contexts, extend their influence by fostering financial networks, industry expertise, and thematic connections across regions. These festivals circulate non-mainstream cinema, establishing alternative circuits that promote global recognition of non-English-speaking films.

McNair and Boumlik contend that Indigenous film festivals engage with political, social, and cultural settings, serving as sites that promote Indigenous representational sovereignty and expressive agency. The authors show how, over the past two decades, Indigenous North African or Amazigh film festivals have proliferated, focusing on relational definitions of Indigeneity and addressing historical discrimination. These festivals have significantly impacted the image of Amazigh culture and influenced film production locally and internationally. Located in a diverse, working-class, multilingual, and multireligious urban community college, NYFAF addresses two main questions: How is a film festival shaped by its cultural focus? How is an Indigenous film festival, like NYFAF, shaped by its location and audience? The authors argue that curating a film festival dedicated to an emergent Indigenous African cinema in a pedagogical setting initiates a journey of discovery, offering a temporary community of cross-cultural encounter and exchange that responds to the target audience, the moment, and to the evolution of this cinema.

In Chapter 5: "Virtualization of the New York Forum of Amazigh Film (NYFAF) During and Post- COVID-19: the Scramble 'To Remain the Same,'" Soubeika Bahri describes how, amid the COVID-19 global pandemic and just like many film festivals around the world, the New York Forum of Amazigh Film (NYFAF) also had to pivot to online and hybrid formats. The virtualization of the film event primarily meant transforming its relationship with the filmmakers and audience and changing the ways its organizers function between each edition while taking into account the pedagogical and transnational aspects of the forum. Drawing loosely on the concept of "scrambled to remain the same" (de Valck and Damiens 2023, 219), Bahri examines online and hybrid transitioning as new strategies and opportunities adopted by the NYFAF organizers to transcend the "spatiotemporal boundaries" (Kredell 2023, 51) and reimagine a future look for this film forum with this new approach. Bahri argues for a different understanding of the virtualization approach and points to the importance of a reflection on the expressions of resilience, disruption, and place particularly in the context of small "genre" film festivals.

Estrella Sendra and Robin Steedman look at the UK's Film Africa in Chapter 6, "From Africa to London to the World: Film Africa's Leading Role in the Circulation of African Cinemas." They argue that Film Africa is currently the largest festival and meeting point in the United Kingdom celebrating the best of African cinema, and they explore what the festival aims to do and how its practices shape the circulation of African cinema in London and beyond. They begin with an exploration of the festival's understanding of "Africa" in dialogue with the festival location. They suggest that the festival adopts an expansive definition, which encompasses the continent, diaspora, and those of African heritage, and show that curating Africa in this way serves as a way of acknowledging, embracing, and celebrating the rich and diverse range of cultural heritages that make up the population of London. They also reflect on Film Africa's exhibition practices in relation to place. The festival is decentralized and hosted across different venues in various neighborhoods. This practice is a way of connecting to the multicultural and diverse populations in London and, very importantly, with the various diasporic communities in the city, while also being a way of bringing other audiences to the cinema. The festival is also curated thematically based on where the films will be screened, and this includes multidisciplinary associations such as curating music events and family activities.

Through reflecting on field research at the festival as well as with its organizers (including reflecting on their own roles within the festival over time) Sendra and Steedman explore how the festival is curated, how the space of London is worked with, and the lessons that can be learned from this festival for other festivals in other contexts.

In Chapter 7: "African Film Festivals: A Transnational Programming Intervention and *Tales of the Accidental City* as a Case Study," Giovana Nabarrete de Souza Cruz and Babatunde Onikoyi examine how, from 2022 to 2023, three African film festivals—Mostra de Cinemas Africanos in Brazil, the African Movie Festival in Manitoba, and Vues d'Afrique in Québec—engaged in an exploratory transnational programming intervention that examined the impact and the perception of a pre-selected film screened at all three festivals. These festivals, held at different times of the year, frame their activities around cultural convergence, connecting filmmakers and audiences, and exploring African living cultural traditions. The authors examine the outcome of screening Maïmouna Jallow's *Tales of the Accidental City* at the three festivals as part of a programming cycle and intervention and demonstrate how the film reached a transnational, multicultural level that highlights the divergence in reception due to cultural context, thus creating a place for discussion between the local public at the festival and the African diaspora. Cruz and Onikoyi examine how the tripartite engagement was crucial to the filmmaker's journeys across continents, as her work met with richly-culturally diverse and transnational audiences, highlighting beneficial cultural exchanges afforded by such a programming intervention—which is, in itself, a curatorial approach.

In Chapter 8: "'Act in Your Location, Think with the World': Constructing Audience 'Afterlives' at Three North American-based African Film Festivals," Sheila Petty and Estrella Sendra focus on three African film festivals/programs located in Canada and Mexico. Beginning with an examination of the longest-running African film festival in Canada—Vues d'Afrique—in Montreal, the authors also explore a relatively new festival in Winnipeg—African Movie Festival in Manitoba, and finally a very recent initiative in Mexico to bring African films to Afro-Mexican communities. Petty and Sendra also look at selected "afterlife" events of the festivals that are organized to build year-round sustained audience bases and community impact based on Bill Reid's notion of artworks (festivals) as "lives" and the community dialogues and events surrounding the works as "afterlives." The authors envision festival afterlives, not in the sense of negative residue of colonialism or slavery, nor as legacy activity, but more as a relationship between filmmakers and audiences and a relationship between filmmakers themselves (Dovey 2015, 100). The network of filmmaker-film-spectator is paramount to building communities and social networks off-screen in local communities and throughout the diaspora. According to Haida artist and master carver Bill Reid, an artwork/film's "real life" is the process through which it becomes a work, but its "afterlife" is constructed during readings of and engagement with the work through shared participation in local and diasporic cultural manifestations (Reid 2000, 71).

We sincerely hope that the chapters in this volume contribute to an on-going dialogue and create a "festival-knowledge forum" that respects the living nature of cultural heritage as it is received from its "original" context and then presented/exhibited, documented/safeguarded during film festivals and passed on to future generations!

Competing Interests This research was funded, in part, by Social Sciences and Humanities Research Council of Canada Partnership Development Grant #890-2020-0102 and, in part, by the Government of Canada's New Frontiers in Research Fund (NFRF) Grant # NFRFR-2021-00161.

References

Allen, Chadwick. 2012. A Transnational Native American Studies? Why Not Studies that Are Trans-Indigenous? *Journal of Transnational American Studies* 4 (1): 1–22. https://escholarship.org/uc/item/82m5j3f5.

Boukouss, Ahmed. 2012. *Revitalisation de la langue Amazighe*. Rabat: IRCAM.

Boumlik, Habiba, and Lucy R. McNair. 2017. Looking for Amazigh Cinema—Developing the New York Forum of Amazigh Film. *Transnational Moroccan Cinema*. https://moroccancinema.exeter.ac.uk/en/habiba-boumlik-and-lucy-mcnair-summary/. Accessed 11 September 2024.

Chan, F. 2011. The International Film Festival and the Making of a National Cinema. *Screen* 52 (2): 253–260.

De Valck, Marijke, and Antoine Damiens. 2023. *Rethinking Film Festivals in the Pandemic Era and After*. Cham: Springer International Publishing.

Dovey, Lindiwe. 2015. *Curating Africa in the Age of Film Festivals*. New York: Palgrave Macmillan.

Gikandi, Simon. 2001. Globalization and the Claims of Postcoloniality. *The South Atlantic Quarterly* 100 (3): 627–658.

Glissant, Édouard. 2009. *Philosophie de la Relation: poésie en étendue*. Paris: Gallimard.

Imorou, Abdoulaye. 2011. Du Tout-monde comme objet d'étude: postcolonialisme, histoire globale et poétique de la relation. *Africultures* 87: 34–42.

Khatibi, Abdelkébir. 1983. *Maghreb pluriel*. Paris: Denoël.

Kredell, Brendan. 2023. Scarcity, Ubiquity, and the Film Festival After Covid. In *Rethinking Film Festivals in the Pandemic Era and After*, ed. Marijke De Valck and Antoine Damiens, 41–58. Cham: Springer International Publishing.

Mbembe, Achille. 2002. On the Power of the False. Trans. Judith Ings. *Public Culture* 14 (3): 629–641.

Mbembe, Achille, and Sarah Nuttall. 2004. Writing the World from an African Metropolis. *Public Culture* 16 (3): 347–372.

Reid, Bill. 2000. *Solitary Raven: The Selected Writings of Bill Reid*, ed. and intro. Robert Bringhurst. Vancouver: Douglas & McIntyre.

Royer, Michelle. 2024. Empowering Oceanic Voices: Francophone Film Festivals and Visual Autonomy. In *Francophone Oceania Today: Literature, Visual Arts, Music and Cinema*, ed. Michelle Royer, Nathalie Ségeral, and Léa Vuong, 63–85. Liverpool: Liverpool University Press.

Open Access This chapter is licensed under the terms of the Creative Commons Attribution 4.0 International License (http://creativecommons.org/licenses/by/4.0/), which permits use, sharing, adaptation, distribution and reproduction in any medium or format, as long as you give appropriate credit to the original author(s) and the source, provide a link to the Creative Commons license and indicate if changes were made.

The images or other third party material in this chapter are included in the chapter's Creative Commons license, unless indicated otherwise in a credit line to the material. If material is not included in the chapter's Creative Commons license and your intended use is not permitted by statutory regulation or exceeds the permitted use, you will need to obtain permission directly from the copyright holder.

CHAPTER 2

On FESPACO Mythology

Olivier Barlet

Abstract Since 1972, the Ouagadougou Pan-African Film and Television Festival (FESPACO) has been like African cinema: a structuring myth. In 2023, a bust of Ousmane Sembène—himself a myth: "the father of African cinema"—was installed at the entrance to the FESPACO headquarters. But is the festival still aligned with the militant objectives defined by the great filmmaker? Whether it is a group of filmmakers or films, these fundamental issues have never ceased to be called into question. The rituals remain unchanged, as does the adjective "pan-African" in the festival's title. What kind of pan-Africanism are we talking about? This mythical notion itself evolves, like cinema, around the question of African identity. Meanwhile, the festival continues to defend its centrality because FESPACO is also a bastion. This chapter examines FESPACO through this lens to consider how necessary this appeal to the imaginary was, and remains, for the African film festival to conserve its top spot.

Translation from the French by Melissa Thackway.

O. Barlet (✉)
Africultures, Les Pilles, France
e-mail: olbarlet@gmail.com

© The Author(s) 2025
S. Petty (ed.), *African Film Festivals and Transnational Flows of Living Cultural Heritage*, Framing Film Festivals,
https://doi.org/10.1007/978-3-031-88590-7_2

Keywords Africa · FESPACO · Myth · Pan-African · Film festival · Burkina Faso

See Fig. 1.

Fig. 1 FESPACO 2023 official poster (Courtesy FESPACO. CC BY-SA 4.0.)

1 Introduction: FESPACO as Foundation

Despite the rise of African film festivals globally, FESPACO remains the main film event in sub-Saharan Africa, and indeed, around the world. The Carthage Film Festival (Les Journées cinématographiques de Carthage—JCC), created in 1966, continues to focus almost exclusively on the Arab world notwithstanding its initially pan-Africanist mandate. The Cairo International Film Festival (CIFF), whose first edition dates to 1920, also gives the greatest prominence to Arab films. The Dakar Film Meetings (Les Rencontres cinématographiques de Dakar - RECIDAK) were held annually from 1990 to 1996, under the direction of the Consortium for Audiovisual Communication in Africa, headed by journalist Annette Mbaye d'Erneville, and then, until 2002, organized by Senegal. They were taken over in 2018 by the then Minister of Culture, Abdou Latif Coulibaly, but did not last. There was again talk of resuming them in 2023, but no follow-up. Created in 1979, the Durban International Film Festival (DIFF) is the oldest and most important festival in South Africa. None of these festivals on the continent, or indeed throughout the diaspora, compete in status with FESPACO.[1]

2 From the Outset, Two Myths in One

Alimata Salambéré, the festival's first president in 1969, has quashed the unfounded theories attributing the creation of the FESPACO to anyone other than Claude Prieux, who was Director of the Franco-Voltaïque Cultural Centre at the time (Barlet 2022a). It should be noted, however, that a group of film buffs from the Centre's film club run by René Bernard Yonli was involved in the realization of the project (Ouédraogo 1995; Dupré 2012). Inoussa Ousseini maintains that Claude Prieux was already considering the idea when, during his previous posting, he was head of the French Cultural Centre in Saint-Louis, Senegal. He shared the idea with Paulin Soumanou Vieyra and Ousmane Sembène, the latter suggesting that he continue to work on the festival project when he was posted to Ouagadougou, promising to mobilize his international contacts (Ousseini 2020). Two points of uncertainty have thus shrouded the festival from the start: its length, on the one hand, with many writers wrongly referring to the *Semaine du cinéma africain* ('African Film Week') when the program in fact indicated the *Festival de cinéma africain de Ouagadougou du 1er au 15 février 1969* ('Ouagadougou African Film Festival, 1–15 February

1969'); and, on the other, the role of Ousmane Sembène, who did not create the festival but did take part in it.

This gave rise to two myths in one. On the one hand, connecting the festival's name to a small event suggested it was a local initiative free of outside intervention that grew of its own accord—the inference being an Africa that rose up with no support. On the other hand, Sembène was no more the father of the FESPACO than he was of African cinema.[2] It was, then, Claude Prieux who set up a sixteen-member organization committee that brought together the workforce and administrative resources needed for a major event.[3]

That said, on the occasion of the centenary of Ousmane Sembène's birth in 2023, a bust of the filmmaker was unveiled right next to the entrance of the FESPACO headquarters, so that anyone entering can pay him their respects. "Identifying those really behind an action is always complicated. Myths are founded because people need them. It's not intentional",[4] stated Filippe Savadogo, Permanent Secretary of the festival from 1984 to 1996 (Barlet 2023). The FESPACO was only given its name on its institutionalization in 1972. This edition was considered the third, however, and it is inaccurate to use the name to refer to the first two editions.

What was at stake, however, was the establishment of Ouagadougou as the headquarters of the Pan-African festival at a time when there was fierce vying between cities: "We above all needed to impose ourselves as *the* place of African film", Filippe Savadogo adds. The threat has never gone away: "Other African countries were about to create an African television festival", he recalls, which justified adding the word 'television' to the name of the festival. "There were even several attempts to take the FESPACO from us, with some countries setting up small festivals in ambush", he continues, before adding: "But the Burkinabè are so welcoming that they would give up their beds and sleep on the floor. The filmmakers knew it".[5] (Barlet 2023). This was needed to make up for the permanent chaos of the festival's organization. As early as 1976, the organization was such that Sembène exclaimed: "It's a fiasco and that's highly problematic!"[6] (Sanogo 1980). Organizational hitches have proven to vary in nature and gravity depending on the editions, but have remained recurrent, with the FESPACO seeming never to have managed to cope with its expansion. The chaos reached its height under Michel Ouedraogo's direction, so much so that the 2009 edition was dubbed the "*Fespagaille*" ('Fespandemonium')! (Barlet 2009a). He attributed this to the difficulty in mobilizing its funds on time and to the sluggishness of "bureaucratic and administrative red tape",[7] calling for the festival's institutional autonomy (Barlet 2009b). "It's not a new demand, but the delegation needs more freedom to constitute its own teams. The failings aren't due to a lack of will, but to a lack of information and overall vision",[8] states Alex Moussa Sawadogo, who has been Delegate General of the FESPACO since 2021 (Barlet 2022b). For the root of the problem remains that, like the Carthage Film Festival (JCC), the FESPACO is one of the few festivals in the world to be state-run, and thus, to borrow Colin Dupré's term, a state affair (Dupré 2012).

3 THE FOUNDING MYTH OF YENNENGA

In 1972, the FESPACO's main award was symbolically named the Stallion of Yennenga in reference to Princess Yennenga and the founding legend of the Mossi Empire. A fearsome Amazon who led the royal cavalry, she became an indispensable war chief, to the point that her father refused all marriage proposals. But the beautiful Yennenga ('the Slender') fled on her stallion. In her flight, she met the young hunter, Riale, with whom she later had a son, Ouedraogo ('the Stallion'). Once he had grown up, she sent him to seek the king's pardon, which the king granted. Ouedraogo returned with goods and warriors, allowing him to establish the Mossi Kingdom.

The festival's anchoring in Ouagadougou was thus affirmed in reference to this legend, which remains highly present given that, until French colonization, the central region of today's Burkina Faso was controlled by the confederation of Mossi Kingdoms. In Eléonore Yaméogo's *Le Galop* ('The Galop' 2023), a documentary parody of competitiveness based on the myth of Yennenga, Aristide Tarnagda's text proclaims: "Genii never sleep; with no competition there are no geniuses, no glory. Every empire needs its genii". While filmmakers dream at least in secret of awards, the film implores spectators to "develop oneself with others, not against them".[9] The festival would have been competitive as far back as the 1970s if it had had the means, but since the beginning it has promoted a façade of unity that is itself perfectly mythical given African cinema's plurality.

4 Under the Banner of the Pan-African Myth

Inscribed in the festival's title, Pan-Africanism has always been part of the program, even if the concept was perfectly mythical in an Africa deeply divided between non-aligned countries and Western outposts, and is one that today remains fragmented, if not to say completely atomized. During the FESPACO's fiftieth anniversary, Alimata Salambéré continued to insist on this Pan-African dimension: "We must hold high the Pan-African flame to remain present in universal culture",[10] she said at the 2019 conference, but without specifying what she meant by the concept (Barlet 2019a). There are two types of Pan-African solidarity: radical and transnational, on the one hand, and internationalist and anti-imperialist, on the other (Mbembe 2010, 21). In film theory, this distinction between a politics of difference and a politics of sameness opposes cinema as an artistic expression with mass appeal and one which also conveys ideology—here ideology being Alimata Salambéré's decolonial and Afrocentric discourse fifty years earlier calling for "an African cinema that addresses Africans; an African cinema made by Africans".[11] (Traoré 2019, 16).

If the aim is "to decolonize screens"[12] (Traoré 2019, 104), to use the now widespread expression, where, with the FESPACO, might this rupture be situated? Thomas Sankara declared in his opening speech at the 1982 conference that "African cinema is still colonized"[13] (Humblot 1982). Since its creation, the festival has programmed films set in Africa but directed by non-Africans (the "Panorama" section), as well as films from the African diaspora. A significant number of diaspora films were programmed in 1985, and by 1989 the Paul Robeson Prize was created specifically for these films. In 2015, however, after lengthy discussions on the Africanity of the films, the Paul Robeson Prize was abolished, and films from the diaspora were then eligible to compete in the Official Feature Competition and thus eligible for the Golden Stallion Award. This was a significant, not to say revolutionary, evolution: territorial categorization gave way to a global belonging to African descent.

For the 29th FESPACO in 2025, the Paul Robeson Prize has been reinstated, and films from the African American diaspora are therefore no longer included in the other categories. Criticism had arisen when the silver Yennenga stallion was awarded in October 2021 to the film *Freda* by Haitian director Gessica Généus, and African American filmmakers, who had always unsuccessfully advocated for increased inclusion of their films (which were virtually absent in 2015), further insisted on improved representation of their own films.

The history of the festival has thus always been marked by the question of the filmmakers' origin. The 1983 FESPACO decided not to select the film *Le Courage des autres* ('Others' Courage') by Christian Richard, a French teacher working at the INAFEC Ouagadougou film school, shot in 1982 by an entirely African crew and starring Sotigui Kouyaté. It was produced by Cinafric, an ambitious Burkinabè private company run by Martial Ouedraogo, which produced several films before going bankrupt (Diawara 1992, 138). It must be said that the film's theme was controversial as it focused on the razzias that certain Africans carried out against others to supply their contingent of enslaved people to the slave ships (Scoleri 2014)—a taboo, as it risked mitigating the horrors perpetrated by white people.

During the Second FEPACI Congress in Algiers, the filmmakers adopted an anti-imperialist, Pan-Africanist charter on January 18, 1975, that came "in the wake of the transformative emergence in world cinema of filmmakers and theorists from the 'Third World'" (Bakari 2020, 294). Denouncing "cultural domination and deracination", they called for culture to be "popular, democratic, and progressive in character, inspired by its own realities and responding to its own needs" (*"The Algiers Charter on African Cinema"* 2021, 53).

In Niamey from March 1 to 4, 1982, filmmakers, critics, government leaders, and experts came together for the first international conference on film production in Africa. The participants adopted what became known as the *Niamey Manifesto* (Bakari and Cham 1996) Unlike the *Algiers Charter*, the manifesto insisted on cinema's necessary economic environment: developing movie theaters, distribution, technical infrastructure, and professional training to improve the viability of productions. It called for television backing and an inter-state cooperation that superseded the national level. It addressed ticketing, taxation, administrative bodies, investment incentives, specialist laws, and co-productions, with participants calling for appropriate legislation.

Shifting from ideology to economics, it was a considerable change of tack, but this was also the moment that Thomas Sankara took power. For this Pan-Africanist icon, the FESPACO was a consciousness-raising tool. Like Julius Nyerere, Sankara believed that Africa should fight with its own weapons. This meant occupying the cultural and ideological realms of cinema, or risk letting the adversary do so. In 1985 and 1987, respectively, the FESPACO themes were "Cinema and People's Liberation", and "Cinema and Cultural Identity". After Sankara's assassination, the also "rectified" FESPACO returned to economic questions in 1989 with the theme "Cinema and Economic Development".

This period of the FESPACO's "unprecedented politicization"[14] (Dupré 2012, 187) saw the filmmakers, Sembène at the helm, demonstrate their solidarity with the Burkinabè people's fight for autonomy by spending a day on the Ouagadougou-Tambao railway construction site, which the World Bank had refused to fund (Boukari-Yabara 2014, 298). As for the new FESPACO Delegate General appointed by Sankara in 1985, Filippe Savadogo was convinced that the festival's survival required "vigorous promotion to turn it into an essential vector of cultural diplomacy",[15] by boosting its continental dimension (Savadogo 2020, 433). The FESPACO's Pan-Africanism was thus above all a logic of unity, a promotion of African unity that increasingly included the African diaspora and its descendants, in keeping with filmmakers who did not remain stuck in a folkloric assertion of an origin, but who worked to forge a new place for Africa in the world (Barlet 2005). Abderrahmane Sissako's reply to Idrissa Ouedraogo, President of the Jury in 2003, was emblematic in this respect. As Ouedraogo handed him the Golden Stallion Award for *Heremakono*, he said: "I hope you come back to us!" To which Sissako replied: "To come back, you have first to have left, and I never have".[16]

5 FESPACO Rituals

Kept alive by "its mediatization and historic aura, the FESPACO's centrality in Africa"[17] needed to be constantly reaffirmed (Barlet 2022b). In short, the FESPACO needed to be made an invincible myth. That notably required the instigation of a series of rituals. The first of these is the first Sunday morning libation ceremony honoring the memory of the late filmmakers, in which festival participants join hands and circle Boubakar Galbani's monument to filmmakers counterclockwise,[18] "in order to represent resistance to the implacable logic of the passing of time".[19] (Sanogo 2020). During his lifetime, Ousmane Sembène would pronounce a few words. In 2003, as warrior-like as Yennenga, he declared: "We are gathered here to remember that we have a very fierce battle to fight, but also to remind us that we are convinced of our victory".[20] (Bosuma 2003, 59). The ceremony always ends with a family photo.

The 1987 inauguration of the Monument to African Filmmakers (a stack of camera lenses, film reels, and canisters) on the former Rond-Point de la Mairie, renamed the Place des Cinéastes in 1985, contributed to the same sense of homage and anchoring. Starting at this monument and running along the boulevard that leads to the cathedral, bronze statues of the winners of the famous Stallion Award have gradually been erected, in a sort of Hollywood Walk of Fame that here nobody walks on!

Every edition of the festival has its own cloth printed with the FESPACO logo. The custom is to quickly get dresses and shirts tailored so that they can be worn in time, not least by the festival stewards present in the professional venues and ceremonies, but also at the cinemas, where percussion bands play before screenings as the audience enters.

The ceremonies follow an established ritual, notably the Special Awards ceremony attributed by multiple juries, in parallel with the official ones. The FESPACO is the only festival where the Special Awards—mainly autonomous from the official prizes and awarded first—hold such importance. They automatically come with prize money attached, and the sums are significant, competing with those of the Official Competition trophies, which are themselves sizable, and are given considerable space in the catalogues and communications. The FESPACO is thus also about money.

The destiny of the Critics Award—a prize that, out of principle, has no award money attached—is interesting. Neither a Special nor an Official Award, it was hard to assign it a place. The possibility of an international critics' award was long discussed with the FIPRESCI (International Federation of Film Critics). After an agreement on an award linked to the prize list was reached, the FIPRESCI designated a jury in 2011. At the airport, its members, and notably the FIPRESCI President Klaus Eder, discovered that their plane tickets to travel to Ouagadougou had not been issued! Before the FIPRESCI's reticence to reattempt this unfortunate experience, but wanting to boost the festival's "cinema" standing, the FESPACO institutionalized the Paulin Soumanou Vieyra African Critics' Award in 2013, attributed by the FACC (African Federation of Film Critics), but as a Special Award sponsored by Radio France International (which previously had sponsored the Audience Award).[21] This episode was significant; film critics thus found themselves reduced to just their African chapter, and that says something about the destiny of a festival whose vocation it is to counter African cinema's marginalization in the world, but which is still not endorsed by the FIAPF (International Federation of Film Producers Associations).

This does not prevent the festival from drawing crowds, however, and strengthening its aura with every edition. Even if the widely cited figures of the early years need to be viewed with caution, it remains a festive event that mobilizes the Ouagadougou public and many professionals and tourists—even if attendance has dropped in recent years due to the threats of terrorism in the region. One only needs to experience the opening ceremonies in the jam-packed 35,000 seat August 4 Stadium to measure the impact. Parades, a gigantic opening clap, equestrian, dance, and laser shows, concerts by famous musicians, and fireworks all ensure the festival's magic. They, like the closing ceremonies where the award winners are announced, are broadcast live on national television.

The opening celebrations then spill out into the whole city, into every local bar, and around the "crafts street", an initiative launched in 1985 to make the festival even more popular. Initially situated on the Avenue de l'Indépendance, then on the Place de la Révolution, and finally near the cathedral and in front of the Maison du Peuple, this market brings together artisans and traders from the entire sub-region.

Covered in posters, the Hôtel Indépendance, the heart of the festival before it was supplanted by the festival headquarters, used to bring "the world of African cinema" together around its swimming pool, facilitating interviews, meetings, and debates in a good-spirited and spontaneous atmosphere. Ousmane Sembène had "his" room there, reserved for him even several years after his death. Heightened by the free or cheap open-air screenings, this conviviality and popular dimension boosted the appeal of the festival, creating the illusion of a triumphant "African cinema" that had found both its economy and market—following which, "African cinema waits two more years to be celebrated again", as Manthia Diawara ironically quipped (Diawara 2020, 53).

6 Mischief-Making Jinns

When the Economic and Social Council decided to take back its headquarters near the Rond-Point des Etats-Unis, work began in 1994 to build a new festival headquarters near Kadiogo Bridge (Sector 2). After many setbacks, it was finally inaugurated in 2005. Specialists in the Burkinabè capital's mystical history warned against this choice of location, sacred woods where ritual sacrifices used to be performed (Cettour-Rose 2018). On January 15, 2013, when construction was underway to tar the roof, a fire destroyed the wooden frame of a new, nearly finished adjacent building destined to house a main screening amphitheater, workshop and meeting spaces, and a spiraling exhibition gallery. Culture Minister Abdoul Karim Sango declared: "This is Africa; the contractors say there are jinns there. What can you do?"[22] (Glez 2018). The construction site was abandoned, and the building left as it was. It was in this abandoned building that Burkinabè Issiaka Konaté shot *Hakilitan* ('Memory in Flight') presented in competition during the 2019 edition. The film depicts an amnesiac professor who gradually rebuilds his life following the flooding of the Ouagadougou Cinémathèque in September 2009. This Mr. Cinema character undergoes rituals led by a spiritual guide accompanied by gothic women. In 2023, Alex Moussa Sawadogo, Delegate General since 2021, organized a scrap metal sculpture exhibition there during the FESPACO, and open-air screenings throughout the year.

7 From Yennenga to #MeToo

It is symbolic that the Stallion of Yennenga Award is named after an Amazon. Omnipresent, this symbol was reproduced on the 2023 edition poster fighting for peace (see Fig. 1). The Golden Stallion Award has never been awarded to a woman filmmaker; however, the Silver Stallion was awarded to Algerian Djamila Sahraoui for *Yema* in 2013, to Haitian Gessica Généus for *Freda* in 2021, and to Burkinabè Apolline Traoré for *Sira* in 2023. The Bronze Stallion was awarded to Tunisian Leyla Bouzid for *Une histoire d'amour et de désir* ('A Tale of Love and Desire') in 2021 and to Kenyan Angela Wamai for *Shimoni* in 2023.

Significantly, the FESPACO has never had an edition theme focused on women. Conferences have been organized: in 1989, *Cinema, Women, and Poverty*; in 1995, *Women's Voices and Visions*. Speeches have paid homage to African women for their endurance and industriousness, for being the mainstay of the family, but more as objects than subjects, objectified by men, and without autonomous subjectivity. It is only thanks to women filmmakers that this conservative vision has been challenged.

In 1991, when no film in competition was made by a woman, a workshop was organized under the auspices of the FEPACI, FESPACO, and the Vues d'Afrique festival in Montreal on the theme of *Women, Cinema, Television, and Video in Africa*. According to Claire Andrade-Watkins, "The workshop unleashed a riptide of emotion, confusion, and animosity which tore across the festival". Debates were passionate, notably because, at the start of the workshop, the chair of the panel asked non-Africans to leave the room, which caused a lot of misunderstanding, and a heated argument "arose on what exactly constitutes an African". Women from the diaspora sent a letter of protest to the festival organizers, who responded with "abashed and embarrassed apologies" (Andrade-Watkins 2020, 204). The workshop ended with a Statement of African Women Film, Television, and Video Professionals calling for a greater presence and consideration of women in African film (Bakari 2020).

From March 3 to 8, 2010, the five-day *Journées cinématographiques de la femme africaine de l'image* (JCFA) festival was launched in Ouagadougou. The festival awarded no prizes, but films received trophies called "the Sarraounia". Journalist and filmmaker Laurentine Bayala published a daily festival news bulletin. For the FESPACO, this constituted a platform for the promotion of African women in film (Ellerson 2020, 65).

At FESPACO 2019, a roundtable convened by the Cinéastes non-alignées association[23] on "The Place of Women in the African and African Diaspora Film Industry" brought together women film professionals, giving them a voice and calling to clean up the sector.[24] Several female actors testified to the harassment they had been subjected to on shoots and the profession's lack of reaction or support. Azata Soro, director Tahirou Tasséré Ouédraogo's second assistant on the series *Le Trône* ('The Throne'), revealed the attack she had been victim of during the film shoot, when she was insulted, hit, then had her face slashed with a broken beer bottle. Judged and convicted for these acts (Ouédraogo 2017), the filmmaker was nonetheless present at the festival to present his TV5 Monde funded work in the official competition. On March 2, the channel announced it was de-programming the series and terminating all collaboration with the filmmaker (Pajon 2019). An online petition initiated by the Cinéastes non-alignées demanded the *Le Trône* series' withdrawal from the competition, but the festival management refused, defending "the independence of the selection committee; works are chosen for their technical and artistic quality".[25] (Douce 2019).

8 Dissension and Challenges

Despite its sought-after unity and pre-eminence, things have not always been smooth at the FESPACO. Disillusion and dissident initiatives have indeed dotted the history of the festival, tarnishing the FESPACO myth.

Recurrent organizational problems have been the source of great dissatisfaction, especially regarding guests' plane tickets and accommodation. The festival seems permanently overwhelmed by its ambition and success, but it is also a victim of its state-run status.

In 1981, critical of their elders, forty or so young filmmakers present at the FESPACO with their first short films created a movement, which they called the l'Œil Vert Collective. They advocated for an aesthetically rich social cinema to radically decolonize film. They wanted "to rely on their own strengths, to put an end to the mentality of being assisted, to set up African co-productions, and to join forces to obtain services".[26] (Bachy 1983, 69). This movement was the object of much discussion but did not materialize into anything very concrete, beyond the production of William Ousmane Mbaye's short film, *Pain sec* (1983).

In March 2000, the Guilde africaine des réalisateurs et producteurs, created in Paris in 1997, published its first Bulletin. Cameroonian filmmaker Jean-Marie Teno was head of publication, and Chadian filmmaker Mahamat-Saleh Haroun its chief editor. The aim of this Guild of mainly diasporic filmmakers was "to bring together African directors and producers in an association to talk more, share our experiences, improve the quality of our films, find solutions for a better circulation of our works, and to at last better defend our interests".[27] They too wished to put an end to the inertia and encourage solidarity.

The Guild's fourth Bulletin (May 2001) was entirely devoted to a searing critique of the FESPACO, its editorial entitled, *A qui profite le Fespaco?* ('Who Benefits from the FESPACO?'). It evoked the festival's "patent ineptitude" vis-à-vis both its guests and the catalogue, the fact that it appeared "not to give a fig about cinema", concluding that "no one was about to sanctify the FESPACO". It also stated that "the festival has not improved over the years, but continues to go from bad to worse", yet adding: "It is because the FESPACO is dear to us that we are upset".[28]

Despite its internal dissensions, the Guild initiated a "Semaine de la Guilde" at the 2005 and 2007 FESPACOs to "encourage new cinematographic visions of Africa". The Guild's online blog was active in 2006 and 2007. The Guild was successively presided by Fanta Régina Nacro in 2002, Abderrahmane Sissako, then Dani Kouyaté in 2006, then from 2011 by Balufu Bakupa-Kanyinda, and attributed an award at the FESPACO. The Guild criticized the poor quality of the FESPACO's selection and its organization. Mahamat-Saleh Haroun, winner of the Bronze Stallion for *Daratt* in 2009, declared in 2011, before being attributed the Silver Stallion Award for *Un homme qui crie* ('A Screaming Man'): "This is the last FESPACO I'll be coming to" (Barlet 2011a).

These two movements: the Guild and l'Oeil Vert, were created in parallel with the Pan-African Federation of Filmmakers (FEPACI), which was accused of inertia or of being entirely driven by a few filmmakers. The FEPACI's rocky history is linked to that of the FESPACO, as it takes advantage of the filmmakers' presence to hold most of its congresses in Ouagadougou.

9 Conclusion: What Kind of Cinema?

Made by a handful of individuals who had to manage everything in the early days, sub-Saharan African's first works were *auteur* films, and the FESPACO was thus an *auteur* film festival. It long resisted commercial cinema, notably the Nigerian video films that emerged in 1992, but its programming came under increasing attack in the 2000s. By then, it included films that international critics considered of mediocre quality. This was seen as an insult to the pioneers, who had set the path for a demanding cinema that experimented in forms capable of capturing African realities and hopes. Was it better to try to win over the public or to develop challenging aesthetic explorations? The composition of the juries and selection committee, which for a very long time was opaque and subjected to diplomatic imperatives, shaped the image of the festival, which went seriously downhill in the 2010s due to the questionable quality of the films selected, to the point that the FESPACO became a "discredited" festival (Barlet 2017).

Alongside the issue of target audiences was another myth that considerably impacted the festival. The pioneers had indeed always declared that they wanted to make films first and foremost for African audiences. Sembène's aim was for cinema to be "a night school", educating the masses. Films accessible to the greatest number were thus necessary, otherwise this would be a "cinema for Westerners". The notion of *auteur* thus found itself challenged, as if *auteurs* are necessarily *auteurist*, intellectual, elitist, highbrow, dominant, etc., when in fact they are first and foremost *metteurs en scène*, "*mise-en-scène* in the sense not of a simple ornamental bringing images of a pre-existing story to the screen, but of a spatio-temporal construction of a world of images and sounds inhabited by speaking, acting, enduring, looking, or dreaming bodies"[29] (Narboni 2024). *Auteurs* conceptualize their films with a whole crew, of course, but remain their creators. *Auteur* cinema can be perfectly popular *and* reach a wide audience.

Both a showcase and a springboard, the FESPACO needed to reconnect with this affirmation of a locally rooted *auteur* cinema. Baba Hama (Delegate General from 1996 to 2008) envisaged creating a FESPACO-bis on odd years devoted to television and video production to recenter the festival on its objective, namely, the promotion of African cinema (Barlet 1998). With his "21 Vision", his successor from 2008 to 2014, Michel Ouedraogo, wanted to turn the FESPACO into a political institution working to distribute African film, rather than just showcase it (Barlet 2011b).

The huge public success of the festival, which culminated at 400,000 spectators under Filippe Savadogo, Delegate General from 1984 to 1996, gradually waned until the "Cannes syndrome", with its red carpets and sharp hike in prices under Michel Ouedraogo finished it off. Appointed after the October 2014 Revolution, Ardiouma Soma managed to put things back on track somewhat for the fiftieth anniversary in 2019 (Barlet 2019b) after its veritable downward spiral marginalized the festival. It was only with the arrival of Alex Moussa Sawadogo in 2021, albeit a professional not from government ranks, that the FESPACO reconnected with its *raison d'être*: a tool professionalizing and organizing the sector that serves as a label for the films selected, while at the same time remaining a festive celebration of cinema (Barlet 2022b).

Today, political instability, the regional security and terrorist threat situation, and a lack of means threaten the festival and make the old dream of an annual FESPACO even less likely, yet the myth that would allow it to be so remains alive; today, more than ever, the FESPACO has the potential to be the soul of African cinema. It still needs to work more on its Pan-Africanism, however, as its workings and organization are still far too Francophone.

Competing Interest The author has no conflicts of interest to declare that are relevant to the content of this chapter.

Notes

1. https://fr.wikipedia.org/wiki/Liste_de_festivals_de_cin%C3%A9ma_en_Afrique.

2. In my humble opinion, when it comes to figureheads, Sembène was more a "turbulent big brother", to paraphrase Erich Fromm, than a protective father.
3. See Wikipedia: Festival de cinéma africain de Ouagadougou 1969, https://fr.wikipedia.org/wiki/Festival_de_cin%C3%A9ma_africain_de_Ouagadougou_1969.
4. "*Les vrais pères d'une action, c'est toujours compliqué. Le mythe, on le fabrique car les gens en ont besoin. Ce n'est pas volontaire*".
5. "*Il nous fallait nous imposer comme le lieu du cinéma africain avant tout*", ajoute Filippe Savadogo. La menace n'a jamais cessé: "*Des pays africains s'apprêtaient à créer un festival de télévision africaine*", indique-t-il, justifiant ainsi l'ajout du mot télévision dans le titre du festival. "*Il y a même eu plusieurs tentatives pour nous prendre le Fespaco, certains pays ayant finalement créé de petits festivals en embuscade*", se rappelle-t-il, non sans ajouter: "*Mais le Burkinabè est tellement accueillant qu'il donne sa couchette et dort par terre. Les cinéastes l'ont bien compris*".
6. "*C'est un fiasco et c'est extrêmement grave!*".
7. "*la lourdeur bureaucratique et administrative des procedures*".
8. "C'est une vieille demande mais il faudrait que la délégation ait une certaine liberté de mettre en place ses propres équipes. Les couacs ne proviennent pas d'une mauvaise volonté mais d'un manque d'information et de vision d'ensemble".
9. "*Les génies jamais ne dorment; sans compétition plus de génie, plus de gloire; à tout empire il faut un génie*". Alors que les cinéastes rêvent au moins secrètement du trophée, le film appelle cependant à "*se construire avec les autres et non contre les autres*".
10. "*Tenir haut le flambeau panafricain pour être présent dans la culture universelle*".
11. "*un cinéma africain qui parle aux Africains; un cinéma africain réalisé par des Africains*".
12. "*décoloniser les écrans*".
13. "*le cinéma africain est encore colonisé*".
14. "*politisation sans précédent du Fespaco*".
15. "*une promotion vigoureuse le hissant comme un vecteur essentiel de la diplomatie culturelle*".
16. "*J'espère que tu reviendras vers nous!*" Et Sissako de répondre: "*Pour revenir il faut partir et moi je ne suis jamais parti*" Abder-rahmane *Sissako, une fenêtre sur le monde,* Charles Castella (52', 2010).

17. *"la centralité du Fespaco en Afrique du fait de sa médiatisation et de son aura historique"*.
18. "Boubakar Galbani: Concepteur du monument de la Place des Cinéastes", https://fespaco.bf/boubakar-galbani-concepteur-du-monument-de-la-place-des-cineastes/.
19. *"afin de représenter la résistance à la logique implacable du temps"*.
20. "Nous nous réunissons ici pour nous souvenir que nous avons un combat très dur à mener mais que nous sommes sûrs de la victoire".
21. https://fr.wikipedia.org/wiki/F%C3%A9d%C3%A9ration_africaine_de_la_critique_cin%C3%A9matographique.
22. *"On est en Afrique, l'entrepreneur dit qu'il y a des génies là-bas. Vous voulez qu'on fasse quoi?"*.
23. *La place des femmes dans l'industrie du cinéma africain et de la diaspora*. Charter. https://www.annalindhfoundation.org/sites/default/files/members/CHARTE%20ASSO.pdf.
24. https://www.annalindhfoundation.org/sites/default/files/members/TEBLE%20RONDE%2029%3A02.pdf.
25. *"l'indépendance du comité de sélection: les œuvres sont retenues pour leur qualité technique et artistique"*.
26. *"compter sur leurs propres forces, en finir avec la mentalité d'assistés, monter des coproductions africaines et réunir leurs forces pour décrocher des prestations de service"*.
27. *Bulletin de la Guilde africain*, n° 1, March 2000, Editorial.
28. "*A qui profite le Fespaco?*", parlant d'une "*incompétence patentee*" comprenant à la fois la gestion des invités et le catalogue, "*se souciant du cinéma comme d'une guigne*", pour conclure que "*personne n'est prêt à sacraliser le Fespaco*". On y lit par ailleurs que "*le festival ne s'améliore pas au bénéfice des ans, mais va toujours de mal en pis...*", pour cependant ajouter: "*C'est parce que le Fespaco nous est très cher que nous sommes amer*".
29. "la mise en scène étant entendue non comme simple mise en image ornementale d'une histoire préexistante, mais comme construction spatio-temporelle d'un monde d'images et de sons peuplé de corps parlant, agissant, subissant, regardant ou rêvant".

REFERENCES

The Algiers Charter on African Cinema. 2021. *Black Camera: An International Film Journal* 13 (1) (Fall 2021): 53–54. https://doi.org/10.2979/blackcamera.13.issue-1.

Andrade-Watkins, Claire. 2020. A Mirage in the Desert? African Women Directors at FESPACO. *Black Camera* 12 (1): 200–207.

Bachy, Victor. 1983. *La Haute-Volta et le cinéma*. Paris: OCIC/L'Harmattan.

Bakari, Imruh. 2020. Towards Reframing FESPACO. *Black Camera* 12 (1): 289–300.

Bakari, Imruh, and Mbaye Cham. 1996. The Niamey Manifesto, 1982. In *African Experiences of Cinema*, ed. Imruh Bakari and Mbaye Cham, 27–29. London: BFI Publishing.

Barlet, Olivier. 1998. Recentrer le Fespaco sur son objet. Entretien d'Olivier Barlet avec Baba Hama, secrétaire général du FESPACO. *Africultures*. https://africultures.com/recentrer-le-fespaco-sur-son-objet-590/.

Barlet, Olivier. 2005. Du cinéma métis au cinéma nomade: défense du cinema. In *Afriques 50, singularités d'un cinéma pluriel*, ed. Catherine Ruelle, 207–214. Paris: L'Harmattan.

Barlet, Olivier. 2009a. Fespaco 2009: Concern. *Africultures*. https://africultures.com/fespaco-2009-concern-10038/.

Barlet, Olivier. 2009b. Evaluation of the 2009 Fespaco, Interview with Michel Ouedraogo, Delegate General of the Fespaco. *Africultures*. https://africultures.com/the-way-to-help-us-is-to-give-us-our-funding-on-time-10049/.

Barlet, Olivier. 2011a. This Is the last Fespaco I'll be Coming to. *Africultures*. https://africultures.com/this-is-the-last-fespaco-ill-be-coming-to-10048/.

Barlet, Olivier. 2011b. The Way to Help Us Is to Give Us Our Funding on Time! Interview with Michel Ouedraogo, Delegate General of the Fespaco. *Africultures*. http://africultures.com/the-way-to-help-us-is-to-give-us-our-funding-on-time-10049/.

Barlet, Olivier. 2017. Fespaco 2017: un festival déconsidéré. *Africultures*. https://africultures.com/fespaco-2017-un-festival-deconsidere-14012/.

Barlet, Olivier. 2019a. Colloque du cinquantenaire du FESPACO: panafricanisme et pérennisation. *Africultures*. http://africultures.com/colloque-fespaco-14640/.

Barlet, Olivier. 2019b. Fespaco 2019: Vers la résurrection. *Africultures*. http://africultures.com/fespaco-2019-vers-la-resurrection-14633/.

Barlet, Olivier. 2022a. *Cabascabo, le film qui a pérennisé le FESPACO*, interview with Alimata Salambéré. *Africultures*. https://africultures.com/cabascabo-le-film-qui-a-perennise-le-fespaco-15294/.

Barlet, Olivier. 2022b. Entretien avec Alex Moussa Sawadogo, délégué général du FESPACO—"Ce que nous choisissons pour le public n'est pas neutre". *Africultures*. http://africultures.com/entretien-avec-alex-moussa-sawadogo-delegue-general-du-fespaco-15295.

Barlet, Olivier. 2023. Histoire du Fespaco: entretien avec Filippe Savadogo. *Africultures*. https://africultures.com/histoire-du-fespaco-entretien-avec-filippe-savadogo-15663/.

Bosuma, Lina. 2003. *Les Aspects rituels du Fespaco*, unpublished BA anthropology dissertation, Université Libre de Bruxelles.

Boukari-Yabara, Amzat. 2014. *Africa Unite! Une histoire du panafricanisme*. Paris: Éditions La Découverte.

Bulletin de la Guilde africain. Editorial. n° 1, March 2000.

Bulletin de la Guilde africain, Editorial. n° 4, May 2001.

Cettour-Rose, Dominique. 2018. Burkina Faso: le Fespaco se cherche un nouveau siège. La faute aux "genies"? https://www.francetvinfo.fr/monde/afrique/societe-africaine/burkina-faso-le-fespaco-se-cherche-un-nouveau-siege-la-faute-aux-genies_3057001.html.

Diawara, Manthia. 1992. *African Cinema, Politics and Culture*. Bloomington and Indianapolis: Indiana University Press.

Diawara, Manthia. 2020. On Tracking World Cinema. *Black Camera* 12 (1): 48–58.

Douce, Sophie. 2019. #metoo en Afrique: la douloureuse libération de la parole des femmes au Burkina Faso. *Le Monde*, May 30.

Dupré, Colin. 2012. *Le Fespaco, une affaire d'État(s). 1969–2009*. Paris: L'Harmattan.

Ellerson, Beti. 2020. African Women on the Film Festival Landscape. *Black Camera* 12 (1): 60–89.

Glez, Damien. 2018. [Chronique] Fespaco: des sorciers pour sauver le cinéma?. *Jeune Afrique*. https://www.jeuneafrique.com/634487/societe/chronique-fespaco-des-sorciers-pour-sauver-le-cinema/

Humblot, Catherine. 1982. Le cinéma africain et les ministres. *Le Monde*, May 6.

Mbembe, Achille. 2010. *Sortir de la grande nuit*. Paris: Éditions La Découverte.

Narboni, Jean. 2024. Les attaques contre le cinéma d'auteur et les "Cahiers du cinema" sont infondées et déplacées. *Le Monde*, March 16. https://www.lemonde.fr/idees/article/2024/03/16/affaire-judith-godreche-les-attaques-contre-le-cinema-d-auteur-et-les-cahiers-du-cinema-sont-infondees-et-deplacees_6222344_3232.html.

Ouedraogo, Hamidou. 1995. *Naissance et évolution du FESPACO de 1969 à 1973*. Self-published.

Ouédraogo, Evariste. 2017. Burkina Faso: Affaire Azata Soro contre Tahirou Tasséré Ouédraogo - Dix mois avec sursis pour le réalisateur de "L'autre mal". *All Africa*. https://fr.allafrica.com/stories/201711140290.html.

Ousseini, Inoussa. 2020. Hasard et nécessité dans l'invention du Fespaco. In *Cinéma africain - Manifeste et pratique pour une décolonisation culturelle: Première partie - le FESPACO: création, évolution, défis*, ed. FESPACO/Institut Imagine (self-published), 117–121. Ouagadougou: FESPACO/Black Camera/Institut Imagine.

Pajon, Léo. 2019. #Memepaspeur, quand des femmes témoignent des agressions sexuelles dont elles ont été victimes. *Jeune Afrique*. https://www.jeuneafrique.com/742656/culture/cinema-memepaspeur-quand-des-femmes-temoignent-des-agressions-sexuelles-dont-elles-ont-ete-victimes/.

Sanogo, Aboubakar. 2020. Ciné-Agora Africana: méditations sur le 50e anniversaire du Fespaco. In *Cinéma africain - Manifeste et pratique pour une décolonisation culturelle: Première partie - le FESPACO: création, évolution, défis*, ed. FESPACO/Institut Imagine (self-published), 209–223. Ouagadougou: FESPACO/Black Camera/Institut Imagine.

Sanogo, Bassirou. 1980. *La longue marche du cinéma africain: le FESPACO, étape essentielle de son développement au plan socio-politique et culturel. Unpublished sociology doctoral thesis*, supervised by Francis Ball, Université de Paris 5.

Savadogo, Filippe. 2020. La dimension culturelle de la diplomatie: l'exemple du Fespaco. In *Cinéma africain - Manifeste et pratique pour une décolonisation culturelle: Première partie - le FESPACO: création, évolution, défis*, ed. FESPACO/Institut Imagine (self-published), 432–437. Ouagadougou: FESPACO/Black Camera/Institut Imagine.

Scoleri, Josiane. 2014. Le Courage des autres. *Cinémas sans frontières*, May 2014. http://cinemasansfrontieres.fr/le-courage-des-autres/.

Traoré, Yacouba. 2019. *Alimata Salembéré Ouedraogo, itinéraire et leçons de vie d'une femme debout*. Ouagadougou: Editions Céprodif.

Open Access This chapter is licensed under the terms of the Creative Commons Attribution 4.0 International License (http://creativecommons.org/licenses/by/4.0/), which permits use, sharing, adaptation, distribution and reproduction in any medium or format, as long as you give appropriate credit to the original author(s) and the source, provide a link to the Creative Commons license and indicate if changes were made.

The images or other third party material in this chapter are included in the chapter's Creative Commons license, unless indicated otherwise in a credit line to the material. If material is not included in the chapter's Creative Commons license and your intended use is not permitted by statutory regulation or exceeds the permitted use, you will need to obtain permission directly from the copyright holder.

CHAPTER 3

Curating Africa in Contemporary Film Festivals in Senegal: An Analysis of the Constellation of Collaborations

Laura Feal and Estrella Sendra

Abstract Seventy years after the first African-directed productions on the continent, the film industry is still precarious. In response, some festivals in Senegal are innovatively networking and collaborating to build capacity and enhance the circulation of both Senegalese and African films more broadly. However, such innovation is still under-researched within film festival studies, particularly in the context of the African continent. This chapter addresses this academic gap through an in-depth analysis of these collaborative forms. We describe them as "constellations of collaborations", a non-hierarchical system of collaboration informally created but

---

L. Feal
Département d'études de Cinéma, Université Gaston Berger, Saint-Louis, Senegal
e-mail: laurafeal@gmail.com

E. Sendra (✉)
Department of Culture, Media and Creative Industries, King's College London, London, UK
e-mail: Estrella.sendra@kcl.ac.uk

© The Author(s) 2025
S. Petty (ed.), *African Film Festivals and Transnational Flows of Living Cultural Heritage*, Framing Film Festivals,
https://doi.org/10.1007/978-3-031-88590-7_3

institutionalized through years of repetition. Drawing on ethnographic research at the Festival Films Femmes Afrique and the Festival StLouis'-DOCS in Senegal, we shed light on the often-invisible links that play a crucial role in the representation and circulation of certain forms of African living cultural heritage. We argue that film festivals in Senegal operate as entangled constellations in film production and circulation.

Keywords Film · Festival · Senegal · Circulation · Constellation · Collaboration · Curation

1 Introduction

Film festivals are crucial agents in film circulation. As films travel to and along festivals, they earn value through awards, words, and experiences by audiences, critics, and fellow festivalgoers (de Valck 2007, 35–38). The importance of those written words and visual images documenting, reviewing, or analyzing the festival is such that scholars have referred to them as "verbal architectures" (Dayan 2000) and "visual architectures" (Damiens 2020, 158–159). Festivals thus act as methods or heuristic devices that allow us to access and understand film cultures. However, festivals are also highly hierarchical structures (Loist 2016) that influence the kind of documentation produced about film cultures and festivals as well as the methods used for archiving this documentation.

Lindiwe Dovey's *Curating Africa in the Age of Film Festivals* is a pioneering effort that addresses not only the documentation of African film festival curation but also the challenges of exhibiting African films both on the African continent and in the diaspora. Although the first film festivals in Africa emerged following independence in the 1960s, African films were "foreigners in their own countries" as most Africans did not have (and still do not have) the means or opportunities to view their films in their own countries (Sama 1996, 148, cited in Dovey 2015, 92). In response to this ongoing precarity in terms of production and exhibition, some festivals in Senegal are innovatively networking and collaborating to build capacity and boost the film circulation of both Senegalese and African films more broadly.

However, such innovation is still under-researched within film festival studies, particularly in the context of the African continent. This chapter addresses this academic gap through an in-depth analysis of these collaborative forms. We describe them as "constellations of collaborations", a non-hierarchical system of collaboration informally created but institutionalized through years of repetition. Drawing on ethnographic research at the Festival Films Femmes Afrique in 2022 and the Festival StLouis'-DOCS in 2022 and 2023 in Senegal, we shed light on often-invisible links that play a crucial role in the representation and circulation of certain forms of African living cultural heritage. "Festivals are never standalone events" (de Valck 2016, 32). We argue that in Senegal, they operate as entangled constellations that create a star system involving not just actors but also filmmakers and other agents involved in film production and circulation.

Festivals become "crossroads of capital" (Adesokan 2011, xii-10), where the social, cultural, and economic capital meet. They offer a unique time and space for the production and circulation of African living cultural heritage. They are a meeting point "where journeys begin" (Adesokan 2011, 10). Akin Adesokan suggests that in the West African marketplace, "roads cross in an endless pursuit of both profit and other things" (2011, 7). Similarly, in festivals, collaborations forge invisible traces unifying where different nodes intersect. Together, they lead to further points, forming a constellation that is crucial to the making of a film economy locally grounded yet internationally situated.

Festivals foster a transnational flow of films and film professionals, which operates as a "passport" for international exhibition platforms, thereby legitimizing the artistic value of these productions. In this chapter, we specifically focus on two festivals in Senegal that work in this direction, namely the Festival Films Femmes Afrique in 2022 and the Festival StLouis'DOCS in 2022 and 2023. Through our focus on collaborations in film festivals in Senegal, we also seek to invite further reflection on contemporary curatorial practices of African cinema in the continent, highlighting a shift from competition to collaboration that could benefit studies on festivals and the cultural industries all over the world.

2 Toward Methodological Proximity: Writing-as-Archiving the Constellation of Collaborations

While acknowledging the multifaceted dimension of festivals and thus the impossibility of offering a fixed definition, scholars have emphasized both their liveness (de Valck 2016) and the social capital involved (Quinn and Wilk 2013; Peirano 2020). According to de Valck, "Festivals take place in the here and now" (de Valck 2016, 9). Visual and verbal architectures, that is, the number of images and written documents released at festivals are extremely valuable, and therefore scholars have relied heavily on them for research (Damiens 2020, 158–159). However, due to the dynamic and live nature of festivals, visual and verbal architectures are somewhat limiting. Digital and printed materials such as brochures, flyers, catalogues, or press clippings are often unable to "account for the unexpected" (Malaquais and Vincent 2016, 199). First, because some last-minute changes take place following the digital promotion of the festival. Second, they are not sufficiently inclusive of the wide array of voices exchanged by live presences during the festival. Third, they do not unveil the multiplicity of connections enabling film circulation.

Such access to a festival's liveness often requires a multi-sited ethnography (Vallejo and Peirano 2017) and, as we have called it elsewhere, a "methodological proximity" toward festival organizers and participants (Feal and Sendra 2021). This works as a telescope, able to give visibility to the constellation of nodes and stars' participation in film circulation. It also consists of writing-as-archiving "nearby" the festival, through a collaborative approach. We, as co-authors, despite being based in Senegal (Feal) and the United Kingdom (Sendra), share diverse forms of proximity that converge in these Senegalese festival sites (Feal and Sendra 2021). Our various lived experiences situate us differently in these festivals, which results in diverse forms of access and activation of circulation of films and conversations around them. These multiple sites of observation, participation, and activation, in and beyond the festival, constitute the multi-sited ethnography through which we produce research and seek to build what is often absent from the archive. In attempting to account for absence, we engage with Lia Brozgal's question: "Can the anarchive be archived?" (2020, 314).

We have applied a visualization method, mind-mapping the various nodes present in two film festivals with distinctly different program focus:

the Festival Films Femmes Afrique (FFFA), founded in 2003; and the international documentary film festival of Saint-Louis, StLouis'DOCS, founded in 2010. The intertwining of these nodes and relationships visualizes a constellation of collaborations, which brings a collective dimension to festivals, benefiting from one another, and building reciprocity practices in the face of scarcity. We specifically focus on FFFA in 2022, and on StLouis'DOCS 2022 and 2023 and we invite readers to engage closely with our constellations, to treat them as living archives still under construction, activating them further as they engage with these festivals. The value of this first analysis of such a complex constellation resides precisely in its way of shedding light on incipient moments of reciprocity still in their early phases.

This methodology allows us to bring in "the ephemeral", archiving it as we write, inviting further scholarly and practical engagement with intangible material made tangible through the written word. As Malaquais and Vincent argue, "[r]ecollections by witnesses—and in particular by witnesses who were not there to cast an official gaze on the proceedings—help fill this gap. Such recollections shed light also on steps in the lead-up to individual festivals that official archives tend to underplay: false starts, failures, and reorientations resulting from these" (Malaquais and Vincent 2016, 199). They also unveil collaborative dynamics crucial to the functioning, circulation, and legitimization of African cinemas.

3   Festival Films Femmes Afrique

The Festival Films Femmes Afrique (FFFA) was founded in 2003 as a result of a collaborative initiative organized through the Senegal-based association Trait d'Union. This association was created in 1997 by a group of French women who shared the experience of having married a Senegalese man and who wanted to better integrate into the local society. FFFA is an illustrative example of the significant role of collaboration in the curation and circulation of "contemporary African screen worlds" (Dovey 2025) in and from Senegal because it is a festival involving many feminists, working on various feminist projects who offer mutual support to one another. The festival espouses a negofeminist perspective, that is, a "feminism of negotiation", with an understanding of patriarchy aligned with the different and intersectional contexts in the continent (Nnaemeka 2004, 360–361). FFFA underscores the challenges faced by women in the industry, involving all genders in the mission to bring women-centered cinema to Senegalese audiences to encourage reflection on the place of women in our societies.

FFFA is the first film festival in Senegal to curate films directed by filmmakers of all genders and nationalities but showcasing strong African women on screen. In the words of the festival itself, as reflected in the submission criteria on the website: "The selected films must tell or document stories of engaged African women who do not give up, who resist injustice and harassment, who free the world, who create and imagine solutions to raise awareness and face difficulties, violence, and everyday struggles. Stories of African women who create solutions for a better future... dedicated to women from the whole African continent and diaspora, celebrating all filmmakers interested in them".[1] This is arguably a polished motto following the curation of the 2022 edition around the theme "Women Creators of the Future", which was celebrated first from 25 February to 5 March in Dakar, then until 12 March across various Senegalese regions and, from 9 to 14 November in Leeds, UK, as a co-curatorial initiative in collaboration with the Leeds International Film Festival (LIFF).

The festival mission is thus not just "educational", as suggested in that same section on the website but also activist (Sendra 2023). Its desired representation of women responds to and resists the historic misrepresentation or absence of women in cinema all over the world while raising social awareness of the need for gender equality, respect, and recognition for women. However, there is a key difference between the Senegal-based festival and its smaller version within the Leeds International Film Festival. In 2022, the opening film in Senegal was *The Great Green Wall* (2019), by the Australian-born American male documentary filmmaker Jared P. Scott. The film focuses on singer Inna Modja's road trip to the Sahel, as she engages in music collaborations while reflecting on environmental issues.

In Leeds, however, the UK-based curatorial team decided to limit the program to films directed by African women directors exclusively, thus seeking to address two gaps in their program: the limited number of films directed by women, and by women from the African continent or its diaspora, although the opening film in LIFF was *Neptune Frost* (2021, Rwanda-France), co-directed by Saul Williams and Anisia Uzeyman. The panel discussion following the screening, on the topic of African Cinema and Cinephilia, allowed FFFA curator, Amayel Ndiaye, the opportunity to share with the UK audience, the curatorial and audience-building approaches in Senegal, referring to the inclusion of directors from different gender and cultural backgrounds to work together toward the same goal.

FFFA shares Ethiopian filmmaker Haile Gerima's conviction that "African filmmakers cannot go on with business as usual without a constant and critical concern for the under-representation of women" (Gerima 2023, 178). With this context in mind, collaboration becomes almost an inherent feature of this activist African film festival. It involves as many people as possible working toward issues of fair and equitable representation and in doing so, fosters a strong trajectory for the circulation of films that challenge "the single story" (Ngozi Adichie 2009). As Senegalese activist and scholar Rama Salla Dieng notes, "African feminists have actively contributed to change the representation of African women" (2021, 9). With themes such as love, everyday forms of resistance, parent-daughter relations, and resilience, FFFA offers an intersectional representation of strong women of African heritage, with agency to challenge diverse power relations within contexts still shaped by colonial and patriarchal legacies.

The first film ever curated for the festival was *Nous sommes nombreuses (There are many of us, women)*, directed by Moussa Touré (2003, Senegal), a long-term collaborator of the festival still involved today. Beyond being a well-established Senegalese filmmaker, Moussa Touré was also the director of Festival Moussa Invite, which ran in Rufisque and Mbao (the outskirts of Dakar) from 2002 to 2014. In FFFA 2022, Moussa Touré was one of the guest filmmakers who attended the opening of the festival and is a regular presence and supporter. This kind of collaboration with established filmmakers who are committed to growing cinephilia endorses the festival, thus contributing to its sustainability over time. Today, the festival prides itself on having achieved the organization of six editions, screening a total of 220 films across different venues all over the country, and having attracted over 32,000 spectators, according to the official report by FFFA (February 2024).

Beyond the film screenings, discussions, and workshops at the Dakar-based Centre Yennenga, a key stellar node within the constellation, FFFA also organizes screenings at Ciné Banlieue. This is a free cinema school founded by Abdel Aziz Boye, now voluntarily run by his disciples in the Parcelles Assainies area in Dakar. It is also an excellent example of a labor of love, inherited from their master, Mr Boye, a constant reference in contemporary Senegalese films. In 2022, the film screened in this space was *Casablanca Beats* (2021), a documentary by Moroccan filmmaker Nabil Ayouch. The film portrays a group of young women learning hip hop from Anas Basbousi, using this as a liberatory tool.

Audiences were welcomed both by a member from FFFA and from Ciné Banlieue. The film was then followed by a discussion chaired by Warkha Samb. This participant adds further nodes in the constellation, since other than identifying as a militant feminist and digital journalist, Warkha Samb was involved in the first *Festival africain du film et de la recherche féministes* (Cinefemfest), directed by activist-scholar Rama Salla Dieng, and which hosted its first edition in June 2023. The presence of FFFA participants (both organizers and audiences) in Cinefemfest is illustrative of the collaboration that enables this festival ecosystem, since in one single festival there are people and resources involved from three other festivals (at least), namely, FFFA, Banlieue Films Festival (organized by Ciné Banlieue) and Cinefemfest. Jury members are also strategically chosen, including, for instance, in 2022, Souleymane Kébé, one of the leading organizers of the Festival StLouis'DOCS, analyzed below. Such an appointment operates as a mutual recognition, legitimization, and endorsement of both festivals.

There are two under-researched forms of collaboration within the constellation of FFFA that work to promote the circulation of women-centered African films. Live embodiment and participation within these spaces are crucial to unveiling them. These are the "Rencontre international des festivals de films de femmes",[2] held on 26 February 2022 at the UN Headquarters in Dakar, and the roundtable "La Voix des Réalisatrices Sénégalaises",[3] which took place on 2 March 2022 at Centre Yennenga in Dakar. The latter was a practice-led case study led by co-curator and chair, Estrella Sendra, who facilitated live online access to the event for UK-based audiences.[4] The roundtable at Centre Yennenga, co-chaired by Estrella Sendra and Ken Aïcha Sy is illustrative of the entangled nodes in the constellation.[5] The opening words of the roundtable emphasized the role of collaborations, explicitly referring to the fact that the idea was inspired by Ken Aïcha Sy's ground-breaking work on creative women in Senegal and the previous collaboration between Estrella Sendra and Ken Aïcha Sy. Similarly, guest filmmakers, Fama Reyane Sow and Dieynaba Ngom, stressed the support received by organizations that facilitated the production of the debut short films they were presenting. These included Ciné Banlieue, in the case of Ngom, and Cinekap and Upcourts Métrages, in the case of Sow. The film credits further refer to having been supported by FOPICA, the Funds for the Promotion of the Cinematographic and Audiovisual Industry from the National Ministry of Culture.

Interventions acknowledged filmmakers and critics like Christian Thiam or Baba Diop, without dismissing the leading role of women in the industry, such as Fatou Kandé Senghor, who was involved in KINO Linguère, an intense filmmaking training workshop for 14 young women which led to the production of two films shot during the festival and screened during the closing evening. This negofeminist understanding of inclusivity set the activist tone of the festival as stated by Ngom during the roundtable: "We can't speak about hope without speaking about people able to create that hope. For me, that is possible if it comes both from women and men. Because we have our identity, and we have our stories to tell" (Ngom, 2 March 2022). The conversation and audience questions showed an eagerness to question the concept of a female gaze, a contested theme that was also addressed in the workshops during the *Rencontre*.

It is precisely the open ending of the live discussion that enables further growth and imaginary traces. Beyond questions and contrasting views around whether we can speak about a female gaze in cinema, there were two further and intertwined themes: the right to self-storytelling and to broaden complex understandings of being Senegalese today. Both Ngom and Sow referred to stories inspired by actual people, about "subjects that concern us", which are inevitably women's issues. The central role of discussion, enriched by the multiplicity of perspectives showcased on screen, is illustrative of the impossibility of defining African feminism(s), and the view that "there are as many African feminisms as African feminists" (Dieng 2021, 10). But the focus on strong women in FFFA is equally insightful of the need "to define our feminism on our terms" (Dieng 2021, 11), opposing sexism, the patriarchy, and exploitation, and addressing context-specific structural problems (Dieng 2021, 12).

The Rencontre illustrated the high degree of local endorsement, even when framing a festival as international. Despite the focus on collaboration with international festivals that have a thematic focus on women, the meeting space had a large presence of local film and festival professionals. These local participants kept the event grounded and connected to existing concerns, discussions, and aspirations shared locally. Participants included journalists, filmmakers, film exhibitors, researchers, and jury members, who asked questions and shared their views with the international guest speakers offering nuances about the context of Senegal.

The participant festivals included the Festival international de films de femmes (FIFF) in Cotonou (Benin), represented by the founding director, Cornélia Glélé; the Festival films femmes méditerranée in Marseille (FFM, France), represented by Karin Oswald, festival director; the Festival International du Film de Femmes de Salé (FIFFS, Morocco), represented by Hicham Falah, curator since 2008; and the host festival, FFFA, represented by the founding director, Martine Ndiaye. The meeting aimed to share practices and reflect on different aspects, organized across four thematic workshops: film training, the film gaze, funding, and opportunities and challenges of creating a network of women's film festivals. In the words of FFFA, the ultimate objective was to "create and consolidate, with the ensemble of festivals, an international collective of women's film festivals, to then invite all women's film festivals across the world, to join".

The shared trajectories and missions unveiled a willingness to advocate for the right to exist. Various initiatives in the continent, namely FIFFS, and FFFA, referred to addressing a gap, since at the time of foundation, in 2004 and 2003, respectively, there were no cinema venues in Salé (Morocco) or Senegal. The fact that the three-year-old FIFF Cotonou was invited to FFFA 2022 shows the inclusive curatorial approach of FFFA. Films and festivals are welcomed and included at different points in their trajectories, enabling multidirectional collaborations that form a constellation.

Chaired by Amayel Ndiaye, workshops included a variety of topics discussed by the participants, who were mainly women from the media and film sectors. They enriched the discussion with contextual information about educational and financial constraints for women preventing cinema from being a truly democratic and inclusive art form. It was decried by the group that there is a whole generation who has never set foot in a cinema venue. Despite the overall consensus that a network would benefit all parties involved, there were concerns about how to sustain this over time in a context of precarity. Participants thought that building and maintaining such a network, sharing women-centered films from across the world and managerial, curatorial practices and resources, would require full-time employed people to manage the network.

4 Festival International Du Film Documentaire de Saint-Louis

The Festival international du film documentaire de Saint-Louis, also known as StLouis'DOCS, is an annual event that brings together professionals and the public in this city in the north of Senegal that has a long film-loving tradition and has made documentary production one of its hallmarks. In 2024, it celebrated its fifteenth edition from 30 April to 4 May 2024. The eligibility criteria stipulate that the films must have been "made in Africa" and/or in "creolophone" territories.

The origins of this complex constellation of entangled collaborations reside in a project piloted by the AfricaDoc network that sought to make Saint-Louis a meeting point and thus a crossroads of capital around "African creative documentary" at the end of the 2000s. StLouis'DOCS emerged as the platform enabling the encounter between African documentary films and their [African] audiences. The festival results from a collaborative initiative between Senegalese production company Suñuy Films and French production company Krysallide Diffusion. Both entities are co-organizers of the festival, each providing complementary added value, mobilizing local, national, and international funds, as well as access to films, expertise, and industry professionals.

For its preparation and execution, as in the case of FFFA, StLouis'DOCS relies on around twenty volunteers, university students, cultural associations, and professionals from throughout the region. This social capital is indispensable in the multiplication of nodes informing and activating this constellation. The event has further developed a network of links with local entities, such as hotels, museums, cultural centers, neighborhood associations, and relevant media and people. These not only contribute to the revitalization of the sector but also the creation of the city. That is, together, through this collaboration, they boost the perception of Saint-Louis as a creative city, as a crossroads of social, cultural, and economic capital, borrowing Adesokan's terms (Adesokan 2011). There is an implied sense of reciprocity in that StLouis'DOCS is not the only force contributing to the creation of the city. The festival itself relies heavily on the collaboration between the city and the different sectors that inhabit it.

What began as a consequence of a "fragility" or weakness in the city, such as the lack of cinema venues, has become a success factor for the popularity of the festival. The public is reached by inviting potential audiences to the festival not only through social networks but also through face-to-face communication. In so doing, StLouis'DOCS is a festival that "develops several strategies to position the festival in the town's imaginary" (Peirano 2021, 60). It also includes a program of school screenings in ten centers including the rural areas of Gandiol and Mpal to build new audiences. In 2023, former student Amina Awa Niang and the director, Maïram Guissé, presented the film *La vie de ma mère* (*My Mother's Life*) at the Ameth Fall Girls' High School. Niang has led the Écrans du Fleuve project based in Saint-Louis since 2023, consisting of a cinema club and a traveling training space. This recent initiative was inspired by StLouis'DOCS with whom she collaborates closely, thus evidencing the mutual enrichment that allows the constellation of collaborations.

Each festival edition screens an average of thirty films, classifying these into the official section and a non-competitive section, which includes the *Resonances* program, showcasing films whose themes relate to the environment; and Panorama Senegal, with a selection of films with a regional focus on Senegal, like *Góom Bu Ñuul/Black Tumor* by Babacar Sougou (2022). Both sections show the sensitivity and continuous work of the artistic committee to access these films, developing relationships of trust with the environment that go beyond the dates of the event and that allow them to be close to the context, building reciprocity practices between humans and inhabited places as a way of rethinking our ways of being in these places. The film *Yaram* (2023) by young director Massow Ka (whose photos have featured on the festival poster for two editions) is a good example, showing the new life of climate refugees, who moved from the fishing neighborhood of Guet Ndar.

By designing this constellation (see Figs. 1 and 2), we contribute to the construction of a living archive that completes the official story, produced before the festival and continuing beyond it (Brozgal 2020). The festival program includes writing residencies, the documentary filmmaking workshop with mobile phones (Pocket Docs), and film criticism workshops, which converge in the official opening or closing ceremonies of the festival. These activities function as another form of collaboration between the festival and new professionals in the sector, offering them technical support and visibility in their work, while helping to generate a proximity network for access to future films.

Participants in these training activities (filmmakers, producers, or film critics) and even those professionals who have broadened their networks

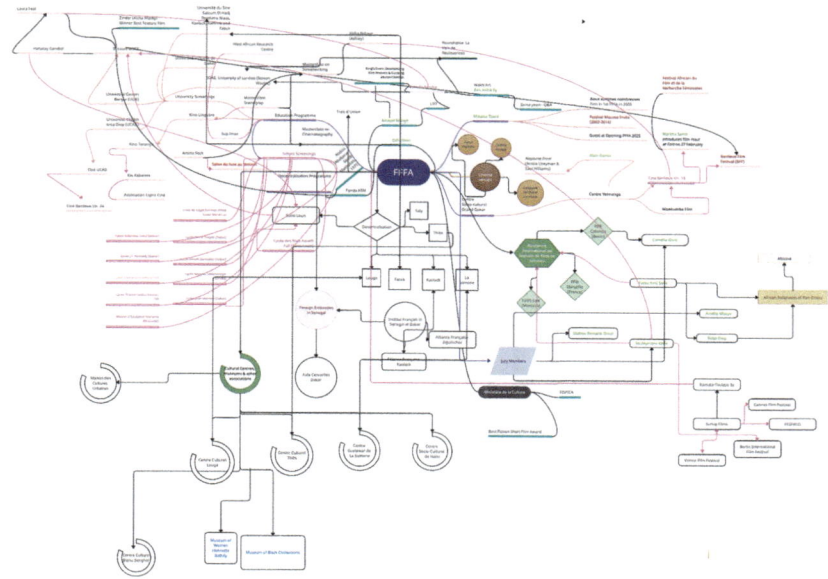

Fig. 1 Visualization of the constellation of entangled collaborations in the Festival Films Femmes Afrique (FFFA) in 2022 (Courtesy Laura Feal and Estrella Sendra 2021)

thanks to these professional gatherings are grateful for the opportunity and feel a certain degree of commitment to the festival. In some cases, this translates into their active participation as trainers in successive editions, such as Mame Woury Thioubou in film criticism. In other cases, this may lead to the premiere or preview of their films at the festival, such as that of Oumar Ba's film *Goufdé* (2023, Senegal). Further forms of reciprocity occur in the festival's communication, with examples such as photographer-filmmaker-film director Massow Ka, who has been involved in various editions in different roles.

These collaborative relationships of friendship and endorsement of the festival by young professionals also facilitate the dissemination of the festival among filmmakers who are outside the most elite international film circuits. They also allow the direct identification of films that could fit into the editorial line of the festival, even when these are not formally distributed. The jury, as analyzed in the case study above, is a key element

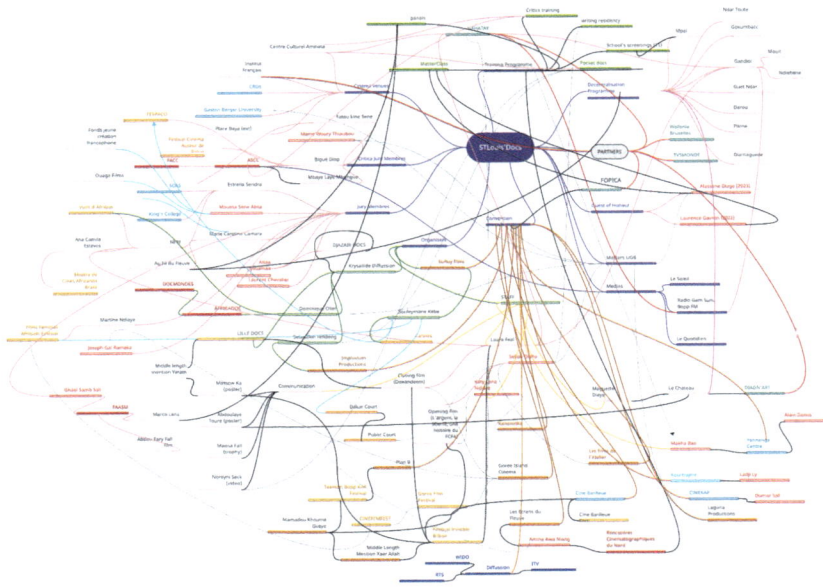

Fig. 2 Visualization of the constellation of entangled collaborations in the Festival StLouis'DOCS in 2022 and 2023 (Courtesy Laura Feal and Estrella Sendra 2021)

in this constellation. It is also one of the few interconnected nodes that give visibility to this entangled network within the written architecture, specified every year in two pages of the festival's catalogue. Directors such as Moussa Sene Absa, Angèle Diabang, Aissa Ben Saïd, Laurent Chevalier, Joseph Gaï Ramaka, and Madji da Abdji; industry professionals; representatives of other national and international festivals, such as Martine Ndiaye, director of FFFA in 2022, and key actors in the city are invited to sit on the jury. The Senegalese Association of Film Critics (ASCC) established its own award in 2021, thus adding "film criticism" value to the films and the festival. Through the presence, endorsement, and support of these collaborators, the work that StLouis'DOCS does, is legitimized, resulting in greater cultural recognition of the films it showcases. This collaboration process adds significant value to the festival.

The StLouis'DOCS encourages the creation of networks with agents of the film industry, boosting the commercial distribution of African cinema.

As observed in the case of Chilean film festivals, they "facilitate securing the attention from the right audience, as well as encountering the most appropriate partners" (Peirano 2020, 66). For example, the *Convention annuelle pour le cinéma documentaire au Sénégal*, established in 2022, was created out of previously held thematic panels under the category of "*Rencontres professionnelles*", the equivalent of an Industry Forum. As part of a political advocacy strategy, the festival succeeded in institutionalizing these meetings in the form of a "Convention" and in involving the Senegalese Cinematography Directorate as co-leader.

The Direction de la Cinématographie, a unit within the Ministry of Culture in Senegal devoted to the promotion of the national film industry, provided an official and institutional dimension fostering hope in the ability of the "Convention" to influence national public policies. As described in the festival's 2022 catalogue, this Convention aims to "create an event that brings together producers, (experienced and emerging) filmmakers, broadcasters, journalists, and training representatives in the field of documentary in Senegal". The Convention was launched at the Mermoz Hotel, where the StLouis'DOCS has its headquarters. There were fifteen participants invited by the organization.[6]

Many of the conversations focused on dissemination, specifically on how to attract attention from Senegalese television stations interested in the documentary film genre. They also revolved around the workshops, training opportunities, spaces, and events that contributed to the development of documentary film production in the country. References were made to key factors including the opening of the Centre Yennenga in Dakar, the training of professional film critics, and the decade in which the Université Gaston Berger in Saint-Louis hosted two graduate (Master's) degrees in production and documentary filmmaking (2007–2017). This training was crucial in the project of positioning Saint-Louis as the African capital of the documentary film production chain, of which the festival is the realization of the last phase, that is, dissemination.

By the end of the discussion, participants suggested the creation of a shared platform of documentary professionals in Senegal, which the organizers of StLouis'DOCS committed to leading. It was not determined how it would be done. However, the fact of mentioning the creation of a shared platform makes us think about the extent to which these decisions are the result of "being" in a collaborative space that can only be in-person and fleeting. These are built through the collaboration of people with similar ideas who create, in turn, "safe spaces" where one can express themselves and dream. This has not yet been realized. However, how feasible is it to subsequently and nimbly produce those ambitious ideas, which arise in the spur of the moment?

On May 5, 2023, a new meeting of the Convention was organized, which would focus on a "production forum" to "develop the creation and production of short and medium-length documentaries". Eight projects were pitched (four by men and four by women), to a panel of thirty experts from training and production sectors.[7] Although the event focused on pitches, the physical presence encouraged more general discussions. Participants talked about the role of emerging documentary authors as ambassadors of "neighborhood cinema" and how their films "invigorate the popular economy" and are only possible thanks to an infinite series of micro-collaborations with local people. These films promote a more real and diverse vision of the multiple Africa (s) that are represented in the continent's cinema and generate new images of their own to put "in circulation and value" in the international market. "What contemporary and endogenous response do we want to give to all the images that for years have been produced of Africa from outside?" asks Professor Mamadou Sellou Diallo, speaking of the place of the Joola initiation rites that the director El Hadji Samba Diedhiou proposes in his project *Fukaraf, la nuit des masques (Fukaraf, the night of the masks)*.[8]

As an example of how this constellation of relationships is reflected in the programming, we highlight *Xaar Yalla* (2020) by director Mamadou Khouma Gueye, screened at StLouis'DOCS 2021. It is a film made within the workshops that take place before the Teemeri Bopp Koñ festival (in Wolof, "a thousand and one corners"), a biannual traveling "political and poetic" event, created by a collective linked to Ciné Banlieue. It is a self-produced short film that probes the issue of the encroaching sea faced by the coastal population of the fishing neighborhood of Saint-Louis. The director not only spent time with the people before filming but also promoted collective scriptwriting and discussion sessions in a traditional format, *pencc*, the Wolof term for "gathering". *Xaar Yalla* was selected for the competition short film section, along with others from national and international circuits. After its premiere in Saint-Louis, it has since circulated in around forty international festivals and, according to its director, "films are made to circulate in festivals, but for their premiere, I always favor places where they have a special meaning, a resonance.[9]"

5 Conclusion

The nature of the participants, along with their shared practices and aspirations, reflect how festivals operate as "crossroads of capital" (Adesokan 2011, xii-10). The collective embodied experience of a festival fosters encounters between social, cultural, and economic capital. The FFFA and StLouis'DOCS exemplify these "crossroads of capital" (Adesokan 2011, xii-10), where the transnational journeys of African films begin. These journeys result from collaborations that lead to further circulation, from one film festival curator to various festivals, digital spaces, and events across and beyond the country and continent. This circulation also involves various actors, filmmakers, cinephiles, and allies who move from one festival to another, often supported by festivals themselves or increasingly by the Senegalese Direction de la Cinématographie.

Illustrated as constellations through an applied visualization method, these crossroads contribute to the creation of a star system promoting a "neighbor cinema", involving actors, filmmakers, distributors, and other film professionals. The curated films offer stories of "affirmation", encouraging discussion on topics that matter locally, nationally, and internationally, both within and beyond Africa. Both festivals aim to add value to their territories, challenging traditional understandings of quality cinema with diverse programs that include highly acclaimed international films and independent films with limited production means, complemented by masterclasses and parallel industry events.

While FFFA offers an intersectional understanding of African feminisms and womanhood, StLouis'DOCS acts as a source of legitimization and valorization of the documentary archive, resonating with the territory and addressing the challenges and aspirations of its inhabitants. Although this is not explicitly stated in the call for films or selection criteria, it is implicitly agreed upon among the organizers and jury. The festival locations thus become centers of local and global reflection on issues that matter to the local, national, and transnational populations, such as the environment, youth, education, women's rights, coexistence, and the tensions between tradition and modernity, among other topics.

Smaller productions are particularly interesting in their function as archives, documenting historic moments, social changes, and intimate visions. These efforts of self-representation resonate with the oral tradition in Senegal, emphasizing filiation, origin stories, the identification of references, ancestors, and education, which serve to ground more private and intimate matters. This makes cinema a key collaborative element in fostering a link between the personal and political spheres, or the body politic. At the same time, the "amateur" films promoted in the programs, placed alongside internationally recognized films, challenge preconceived ideas of cinema among audiences in Senegal, bringing further themes and styles to the screen. The result is a pluriversal and intersectional representation of the diversity within the African continent, with increasing openness to Creole territories.

Collaboration is crucial to the circulation of a universal Africa. It multiplies the range of nodes within the constellation, and the allies committed to the circulation of African cinemas. There is a view that the more people join and endorse the project, the larger the impact it can have. Festivals become safe spaces through which to share aspirations and dreams prompted by the magic of the embodied shared space. While there are acknowledged challenges in materializing such dreams, the resulting constellation fosters a transition from intangibility to tangibility, which is key to building the creative industry in Senegal.

Competing Interests Part of the research for this chapter draws on research funded by Social Sciences and Humanities Research Council of Canada and developed through Partnership Development Grant #890–2020-0102 and the Government of Canada's New Frontiers in Research Fund (NFRF) Grant # NFRFR-2021–00161.

Notes

1. See the website at https://www.filmsfemmesafrique.com/. In its original language, French: "Les films sélectionnés devront raconter ou documenter des histoires qui parlent de femmes africaines engagées qui ne se résignent pas, qui résistent aux injustices et au harcèlement, qui libèrent la parole, qui créent et imaginent des solutions pour sensibiliser et faire face aux difficultés, violences et luttes auxquelles elles sont confrontées au quotidien. Des histoires de femmes africaines qui créent des solutions pour un avenir meilleur…- consacrés aux femmes de toute l'Afrique et de la diaspora et à célébrer les cinéastes qui s'y intéressent".
2. This can be translated as 'International Meeting of Women Film Festivals'.

3. This was translated as 'Decolonising Film with African Women Filmmakers' for UK-based online audiences, in order to be coherent with a wider program of events by Screen Worlds.
4. This event thus involved an international collaborator, the European Research Council funded research project African Screen Worlds: Decolonising Film and Screen Studies at SOAS, University of London, directed by Professor Lindiwe Dovey, a connection made by Estrella Sendra, which would then lead to further connections between some of the festival organizers and Higher Education Institutions based in the United Kingdom and Canada. For example, Amayel Ndiaye was invited to a film and discussion event at King's College London, where she met with Lindiwe Dovey and further curators and researchers of African film festivals. The event, hosted in March 2023, included the screening of *Astel*, a short film directed by Ramata-Toulaye Sy (Senegal), produced by Souleymane Kébé, (co-organiser of StLouis'DOCS), presented and discussed by Amayel Ndiaye (Sendra 2023).
5. A video of the roundtable has been uploaded, with minor editing, as part of the visual architectures of this festival.
6. Participants were from Gaston Berger University (UGB) of Saint-Louis (department of Arts and Culture Crafts, UFR-CRAC), Ciné Banlieue (Collective of filmmakers, artists and cinephiles dedicated to cinema and its learning, based in the periphery of Dakar and created in 2008 by Abdel Aziz Boye, https://cinebanlieue dakar.com/), Yennenga Center (Hub dedicated to film training, creation and dissemination, created in Dakar by director Alain Gomis. https://www.centreyennenga.com/), Forut Média Center (Training center for audiovisual trades (marketing, graphics, cinema) located in Dakar https://mediacentredakar.com/site/), Les films de l'Atelier (Created by UGB film professors, Gora Seck and Sellou Diallo, accompany young filmmakers in the writing, production and dissemination phases http://www.africine.org/structure/films-de-latelier-les/3020) and the Kourtrajmé Dakar school (Collective of artists audiovisuals created in 1994 by Kim Chapiron, Romain Gavras and Toumani Sangaré, with the aim of "dynamizing film production". In 2020 a new training center opens in Dakar https://ecolekourtrajmedakar.sn/).
7. CinéKap (independent production structure based in Dakar, founded and directed by Oumar Sall that aims to create a

network of young authors and directors, "anchor of the renewal of cinema in Senegal" https://cinekap.com/), Les Films de l'Atelier, Gorée Island Cinéma (production company based on the island of Gorée, founded by director Joseph Gaï Ramaka https://www.goreecinema.com/), Impluvium productions (production company created by Sebastien Tendeng, one of the initiators of the StLouis'- DOCS festival in Dakar https://www.facebook.com/Impluvium Prod/?locale=fr_FR), Karoninka (Production company created by the director Angele Diabang, member of the artistic committee of the festival https://www.facebook.com/Karoninka.films/), Lagune Images Productions (Production company based in Saint-Louis, by former students of the UGB master's degree https://www.facebook.com/Laguneprod/), Plan B Films (Society production and accompaniment based in Pink Lake, Dakar https://www.facebook.com/PLANBFILM/), Suñuy Films, Salndu (Cultural company created in 2019 by the producer Tabara Ly, which highlights, in particular, the puular language), L'Écran du Fleuve, Ciné Banlieue, Center Yennenga, Forut Media Center), and broadcast (ITV Chain of the Emedia group (iRadio / iTV / Emedia.sn / Bes Bi quotidien)., RTS (Radio Television Senegalese, public) and Wido (mobile application that allows access to exclusive audiovisual content).
8. Production Forum Meeting, Mermoz hotel, May 5, 2023.
9. Interviewed by Laura Feal 27.01.24.

References

Adesokan, Akinwumi. 2011. *Postcolonial Artists and Global Aesthetics*. Bloomington: Indiana University Press.

Adichie, Chimamanda Ngozi. 2009. The Danger of a Single Story. https://www.youtube.com/watch?v=D9Ihs241zeg. Accessed 15 June 2024.

Brozgal, Lia. 2020. *Absent the Archive: Cultural Traces of a Massacre in Paris, 17 October 1961*. Liverpool: Liverpool University Press.

Damiens, Antoine. 2020. *LGBTQ Film Festivals: Curating Queerness*. Amsterdam: Amsterdam University Press.

Dayan, Daniel. 2000. Looking for Sundance: The Social Construction of a Film Festival. In *Moving Images, Culture and the Mind*, ed. Ib. and Bondebjerg, 43–52. Luton: University of Luton Press.

De Valck, Marijke. 2007. *Film Festivals: From European Geopolitics to Global Cinephilia*. Amsterdam: Amsterdam University Press.

De Valck, Marijke. 2016. 'Introduction: What is a film festival? How to study festivals and why you should?' In *Film Festivals: History, Theory, Method, Practice*, edited by de Valck, Marijke, Kredell Brendan, and Skadi Loist, 24–38. London and New York: Routledge.

Dieng, Rama. 2021. *Féminismes africains, une histoire décoloniale*. Paris: Présence Africaine.

Dovey, Lindiwe. 2015. *Curating Africa in the Age of Film Festivals*. New York: Palgrave Macmillan.

Dovey, Lindiwe, Añulika Agina, and Michael W. Thomas. 2025. *Contemporary African Screen Worlds*. Durham: Duke University Press.

Feal, Laura, and Estrella Sendra. 2021. Nearby the Festival International du Film Documentaire de Saint-Louis: Rethinking Proximity in Times of Covid-19. *NECSUS, European Journal of Media Studies* 10: 261–273.

Gerima, Haile. 2023. Where Are the African Women Filmmakers? In *African Cinema: Manifesto and Practice for Cultural Decolonization*, ed. Michael T Martin and Gaston Jean-Marie Kaboré, 176–183. Bloomington: Indiana University Press.

Loist, Skadi. 2016. The Film Festival Circuit: Networks, Hierarchies and Circulation. In *Film Festivals: History, Theory, Method, Practice*, ed. Marijke de Valck, Brendan Kredell, and Skadi Loist, 49–64. London: Routledge.

Malaquais, Dominique, and Cédric. Vincent. 2016. Panafest: A Festival Complex Revisted. In *The First World Festival of Negro Arts, Dakar 1966*, ed. David Murphy, 194–202. Liverpool: Liverpool University Press.

Nnaemeka, Obioma. 2004. Nego-Feminism: Theorizing, Practicing and Pruning Africa's Way. *Signs* 29 (2): 360–378.

Peirano, María Paz. 2020. Mapping Histories and Archiving Ephemeral Landscapes: Strategies and Challenges for Researching Small Film Festivals. *Studies in European Cinema* 17 (2): 170–184.

Peirano, María Paz. 2021. Between Industry Labs and Audience Formation: Film Festivals and the Transformation of the Field of Film Production in Chile. *Society and Leisure* 44 (1): 47–65.

Quinn, Bernadette, and Linda Wilks. 2013. "Festival Connections: People, Place and Social Capital." In *Exploring the Social Impacts of Events* edited by Richards, Greg, de Brito, Marisa, and Wilks, Linda, 1st ed. Oxon: Routledge, pp. 15–30.

Sendra, Estrella. 2023. Traveling to Audiences: The Decentralization of Festival Spaces at the Festival Films Femmes Afrique in Senegal. *Journal of Festive Studies* 5: 304–325.

Vallejo, Aida, and María Paz Peirano. 2017. *Film Festivals and Anthropology*. Cambridge: Cambridge Scholars Publishing.

List of Films Cited

Casablanca Beats. 2021. Dir. Nabil Ayouch. Morocco, France. 102 min. Les Films du Nouveau Monde. Available from Curzon Home Cinema. https://homecinema.curzon.com/film/casablanca-beats/.

Goufdé. 2023. Dir. Oumar Ba. Senegal, France. 55 min. Vies des Hauts Production. Available from TV5 Monde Afrique. https://afrique.tv5monde.com/videos/goufde.

Góom Bu Ñuul/Black Tumor. 2022. Dir. Babacar Sougou. Senegal. 20 min. Média Centre de Dakar. Not available online.

The Great Green Wall. 2019. Dir. Jared P. Scott. US. 90 min. Wazabi Films. Available from YouTube. https://www.youtube.com/watch?v=PDntErosMD4

Neptune Frost. 2021. Dir. Saul Williams and Anisia Uzeyman. 105 min. Swan Films. Available from Amazon.

Nous sommes nombreuses /There are many of us, women. 2003. Dir. Moussa Touré. Senegal. Not available online.

La vie de ma mère / My mother's life. Dir. Maïram Guissé. France. 52 min. Sudu Connexion. Not available online.

Xaar Yalla. 2020. Dir. Mamadou Khouma Gueye. Senegal. 26 min. Plan B Films. Not available online.

Yaram. 2023. Dir. Massow Ka. Senegal. 25 min. Ndar Nataal Studio. Not available online.

Open Access This chapter is licensed under the terms of the Creative Commons Attribution 4.0 International License (http://creativecommons.org/licenses/by/4.0/), which permits use, sharing, adaptation, distribution and reproduction in any medium or format, as long as you give appropriate credit to the original author(s) and the source, provide a link to the Creative Commons license and indicate if changes were made.

The images or other third party material in this chapter are included in the chapter's Creative Commons license, unless indicated otherwise in a credit line to the material. If material is not included in the chapter's Creative Commons license and your intended use is not permitted by statutory regulation or exceeds the permitted use, you will need to obtain permission directly from the copyright holder.

CHAPTER 4

Journeys of Discovery: The Case of the New York Forum of Amazigh Film (NYFAF)

Lucy R. McNair and Habiba Boumlik

Abstract Over the past two decades, Indigenous North African or Amazigh film festivals have proliferated, focusing on relational definitions of Indigeneity and addressing historical discrimination. These festivals have significantly impacted the image of Amazigh culture and influenced film production locally and internationally. This chapter provides a case study of the New York Forum of Amazigh Film (NYFAF), founded in 2015 and co-curated by the authors. Located in a diverse, working-class, multilingual, and multi-religious urban community college, NYFAF addresses two main questions: How is a film festival shaped by its cultural focus? How is an Indigenous film festival, like NYFAF, shaped by its location and audience? The authors argue that curating a film festival dedicated to an emergent Indigenous African cinema in a pedagogical

L. R. McNair (✉) · H. Boumlik
LaGuardia Community College, New York, NY, USA
e-mail: lmcnair@lagcc.cuny.edu

H. Boumlik
e-mail: hboumlik@lagcc.cuny.edu

© The Author(s) 2025
S. Petty (ed.), *African Film Festivals and Transnational Flows of Living Cultural Heritage*, Framing Film Festivals,
https://doi.org/10.1007/978-3-031-88590-7_4

setting initiates a journey of discovery, offering a temporary community of cross-cultural encounter and exchange that responds to the target audience, the moment, and to the evolution of this cinema.

Keywords NYFAF · Amazigh · Indigenous · Film · Festival · Journey · Discovery

1 Introduction

The phenomenon of the culturally focused film festival is often deeply rooted in local or regional milieus yet extends its influence on a broader scale by fostering financial networks, industry expertise, and thematic connections across geographical areas. Forging links between arts and media, film festivals also permit the circulation of non-mainstream cinema products, including short films, videos, and social media formats. According to Turan (2002, 8), they establish an alternative circuit in a given location that nourishes the recognition of "foreign language" or non-English-speaking films and filmmakers, contributing to what Wong calls "global film culture" (2011, 18) and what Bill Nichols has termed "traffic in cinema" (1994, 68).

Within this context, Indigenous film festivals represent a distinctive category due to their objectives and structure. Often closely intertwined and engaged with the political, social, and cultural settings in which the films are set, these performative and dialogic "anthropological sites" (Severs 2019) or "sites of persuasion" (Howard Morphy 2006, cited in Graham and Penny 2014, eBook) engage local and broader publics with contemporary modes of establishing and legitimizing "Indigenous representational sovereignty", a term that describes the ways Indigenous peoples gain expressive agency and choose to represent their worlds (Wilson 2016, 97). To some degree, these festivals also adhere to the principles of networking, dissemination, and building prestige, often driven by academic interest in the films and cultures showcased or an activist agenda (Severs 2019).

Over the past two decades, Indigenous North African or Amazigh film festivals have proliferated in North Africa, Europe, and North America, inside and outside the historical geographical borders of Berber or Amazigh communities, also known as *Tamazgha*.[1] Their purpose and actions are complex. On the one hand, they endeavor to identify, collect, and screen a nascent body of cinematic work that they identify as belonging to Amazigh cinema, focusing less on territorial than on (re)emergent, relational definitions of North African Indigeneity or Amazighity.[2] Through the festival lens, they actively showcase the societies these films portray and within which they are made (Merolla et al. 2019; McNair and Laayouni 2021). On the other hand, they respond in different ways to a history of discrimination against Amazigh languages and cultural expression in favor of local and regional Arab nationalist ideologies, especially during the period of decolonization and nation-building that extended into the late 1980s. As a result, these regional and diasporic festivals have grown to have a socially important impact on the image of Amazigh culture both locally and internationally, and, in turn, on the nature of film production itself.

To shed light on this layered subject, we will focus on the New York Forum of Amazigh Film or NYFAF (www.nyfaf.com) founded in 2015 by co-author Habiba Boumlik, co-curated by both authors and held annually at LaGuardia Community College, part of the City University of New York. Located in an urban community college with a diverse, working-class, multilingual and multi-religious population, NYFAF also takes place in a country and region with complex collective experiences and associations with Indigeneity. Taking this local context into account, our chapter will address two main questions: How is a film festival shaped by its cultural focus? Secondly, how is an Indigenous film festival, such as NYFAF, shaped by its location and audience? We argue that the process of curating a film festival dedicated to an emergent Indigenous African cinema, in a place that is far from and unfamiliar with this culture and the problematics of its representation in film including production and distribution hurdles, initiates and requires a journey of discovery. In turn, due to our location and audience, this journey of discovery shapes and enriches a parallel pedagogically driven, adaptive perspective on the films, leading the festival to offer a temporary community of cross-cultural encounter and exchange that responds to the moment and to the evolution of this cinema.

2 Film Festival Research and Indigenous Film Festivals

Film festivals play a significant role in enhancing the value of cinema on the periphery. As films move through the festival circuit, they can accumulate symbolic value. The greater the number of accolades, awards, and recognition a film garners, the more likely it is to attract attention at other film festivals. Consequently, filmmakers accrue growing prestige as their works circulate within these events (Peirano 2017, 4).

Whatever the focus of a film festival, its role as a cultural phenomenon has served as a starting point for scholarly study, which increasingly examines these events as sites of important and complex "intersemiotic translation"—moving between locations, languages and mediums—and as decolonizing cultural products and practices in themselves (McNair and Laayouni 2021). Indeed, research on film festivals has seen a substantial surge in interest since the mid-2000s, initially influenced by Bill Nichols' 1994 essay "Global Image Consumption in the Age of Late Capitalism" which established that film festivals as a circuit of distribution "allow the local to circulate globally within a specific system of institutional assumptions, priorities, and constraints" (68). Encouraging audiences to infer meanings, acknowledge difference, and cultivate "a sense of humility, curiosity and receptivity", film festivals offer people a space of intercultural discovery where "a set of encoded meanings [is] rendered intelligible" (Nichols 1994, 69). Building on Nichols' early work, film festival research has evolved into an interdisciplinary field as shown in the breadth of work circulated by the Film Festival Research Network (www.filmfestivalresearch.org) (Peirano 2017, 3).

In the early stages of film festival studies, a primary challenge was to categorize various festival types and to identify their unique functions and attributes, targeting the multiple facets of a film festival (Papadimitriou and Ruoff 2016, 1). Key questions addressed include: How do festivals operate? Can the historical development of festivals be divided into distinct phases? What is the purpose behind their existence? Who are the key actors involved? What is their impact? In recent times, there has also been growing concern about the proliferation of as well as the future or survival of such festivals.

We wish to link these questions to the context of Indigenous film festivals, and to festivals that highlight Indigenous North African film expression, that has often been absent in studies of African cinema. In her thesis "Visual Sovereignty and Indigenous Film Festivals: A Case Study on The Native Crossroads Film Festival", Caitlin Severs posits that such film festivals can be studied as "anthropological sites" (2019, 24). She identifies 67 Indigenous film festivals worldwide.[3] Severs also highlights that from an anthropological standpoint, the collection of Indigenous films showcased at these festivals creates an opportunity to explore cultural interactions between Indigenous filmmakers and both Indigenous and non-Indigenous audiences, exchanges that can take place regardless of the audience's primary composition. For instance, at the Native Crossroads Film Festival, a joint effort of the University of Oklahoma, The Chickasaw Nation, and local arts organizations, films from around the world are presented, but the majority of the audience comprises Indigenous individuals from Native American First Nations in Oklahoma and Indigenous students from different states. Therefore, Indigenous audience members actively learn about the experiences, challenges, and viewpoints of other Indigenous communities worldwide while gaining insights into the potential of Indigenous media.

In Latin America, numerous Indigenous film festivals are held, operating autonomously and frequently in partnership with anthropology schools, local museums, and national and international cultural organizations (Peirano 2017, 79). These festivals primarily focus on showcasing the creations of Indigenous media producers, encompassing works by non-Indigenous filmmakers that address Indigenous concerns. Indigenous festivals often feature auto-ethnographic films aimed at bringing attention to issues of immediate importance to Indigenous communities.

According to Maria Paz Peirano, the oldest anthropological film festival in Latin America (Argentina 1991) aims to spread the works of filmmakers among audiences interested in "the social construction of identity", (79) including works on Indigenous peoples and other ethnic groups, traditional festivities, and local socio-political issues. Some film festivals are well-established[4] and often include academic and cultural events such as conferences, roundtables, workshops, photography, and art exhibitions. For instance, the Jornadas de Antropología Visual de Mexico was created as a cultural academic event, which integrated an academic symposium with retrospectives. This process bears some similarities with the inception of NYFAF, as discussed below. There are ongoing efforts to establish more regional connections between these endeavors (Peirano 2017, 78).[5]

3 Amazigh Film and Film Festivals

Amazigh or Imazighen in plural refers to the native peoples of North Africa. Of Muslim, Christian, Jewish, and animist faiths, they have lived as farmers, craftspeople, and merchants in these lands between sea and desert for millennia. Today they represent a culturally diverse example of Indigenous communities within the larger Semitic world who strive to maintain their cultural, spiritual, and linguistic practices despite sectarian nationalism and a conservative understanding of Islam. Due to the Arab-centric state and social frameworks in these countries post-independence, films in Amazigh languages depicting Amazigh ways of life were banned in North Africa until the 1990s, when a vibrant amateur video and film production emerged, exploring the human dramas of childhood and family life, the struggle for education, stock characters and tales of oral tradition, and the common experience of emigration. What is often cited as the first short film, Cherif Aggoune's *La fin des djinns (The End of the Genies)*, was produced in 1990 (Devaux Yahi 2017). However, faced with the financial constraints of using 35 mm film and the absence of government support, most independent Amazigh filmmakers initially chose the more cost-effective and portable format of video that enabled them to reach even the most remote areas and a broader audience (Carter 2001, 250). Some research has connected the rise of Amazigh film festivals to initiatives aimed at recognizing the emergence of such under-supported visual media and a shared commitment to safeguard endangered languages and Indigenous ways of life in North Africa (Soussi 2019).

Following significant forays into the realm of directing and producing video films, numerous Amazigh producers and directors, including Abderrahmane Bouguermouh (*The Forgotten Hill*, Algeria, 1996), Belkacem Hadjadj (*Machaho*, Algeria, 1996), Azzedine Meddour (*Mountain of Baya*, Algeria, 1997), and Mohamed Mernich (*Tilila*, Morocco, 2006), then decided to take the leap into mainstream feature-length films. With a surge in Amazigh video and cinematic productions during the late 1990s—which Amazigh Studies scholar Daniela Merolla refers to as "Amazighwood" (Merolla 2020) and Amazigh scholar and writer Brahim El Guabli suggests we see in a larger cultural flowering that he names "Amazighitude" (El Guabli 2021)—the necessity for organizing Amazigh film festivals became apparent, particularly since national and local festivals did not cater to the selection and inclusion of Amazigh films often based on Amazigh language scenarios and social dramas.

As film distributors are rarely integrated into the production process, in contrast to countries with well-established film industries, Amazigh film festivals thus came to play a central role in promoting Amazigh cinema. The concept of organizing an inaugural Amazigh film festival began to take shape in Casablanca, Morocco, hosted by AMREC,[6] the first Amazigh NGO, in July 2000, a decade after the release of the first Amazigh film. This early event received support from the Ministries of Culture and Communication, the Moroccan Cinema Center (CCM), and various Amazigh cultural organizations. It featured a lineup that included Moroccan and Algerian Amazigh films. Over the past two decades, the number of festivals dedicated to Amazigh cinema has grown significantly, with more than thirteen such festivals, some of which take place in North Africa, but also in France, Canada, and the United States. Many of them were initiated by members of North African diasporas.

In addition to NYFAF, the most important Amazigh film festivals are the "Festival Issni N'Ourgh International du Film Amazigh" (FINIFA) held annually since 2007 in Agadir (Morocco); "Festival Rif du Film Amazigh" organized by "L'atelier Cinématographique" in Tetouan (Morocco); "Festival Culturel National du Film Amazigh" (FCNFA) held in Tizi-Ouzou (Algeria); "Festival Tafsut pour le Cinéma Amazigh Maghrébin" held in Tafraout (Morocco); "Amazigh Film Festival of Boston" (USA); "Amazigh Film Festival of Los Angeles" organized by Tazzla Institute (USA); "Festival International du Film Amazigh de Montréal" (Canada); "Festival International des Films Berbères de Paris" organized by Berber TV in Paris (France); and finally "Les Journées Internationales du Film Amazigh" (JIFA) in Ars-sur-Moselle (France).

These significant Amazigh festivals serve as platforms where stakeholders in Amazigh cinema, as well as Amazigh activists and artists, aim to affirm their unique artistic identity while also fostering opportunities for interaction and professional inspiration. Apart from presenting films, certain festivals provide supplementary offerings to both participants and audiences. These events may encompass conferences, meetings, symposia, workshops, feedback sessions, training programs, a video library that allows individual viewing of selected festival films, and, eventually, archival services. These gatherings also serve as valuable platforms for enhancing the skills of emerging filmmakers through scholarships, grants, scripts readings, project competitions, and connecting project creators with potential funding and producers. Collectively, they promote the dissemination of films in the Maghreb region and worldwide, while helping

Fig. 1 Poster for the 2017 3rd edition of New York Forum of Amazigh Film (NYFAF) (Courtesy New York Forum of Amazigh Film)

establish a professional framework within the global film and audiovisual industry. Additionally, they offer a preview platform for producers to showcase their films and spotlight emerging talent. In these ways, national and international Amazigh film festivals play a crucial role in promoting film production and addressing obstacles in the development of the Amazigh film industry. Ultimately, they contribute to the reinvigoration of the Amazigh language, culture, and identity in the Maghreb and beyond. Sadly, however, the growth of film festivals has been limited by restricted access to financial resources and the underdevelopment of film industries in these home countries. As a result, the sustainability of Amazigh film festivals is notably constrained (Fig. 1).

4 Case Study: The New York Forum of Amazigh Film or NYFAF

In the Little Theater of the LaGuardia Performing Arts Center or LPAC, located in Queens, New York, a borough famous for its culinary and linguistic diversity, there are 200 seats, a tech box, and a stage. Physically attached to LaGuardia Community College, a Hispanic-serving institution of some 12,000 full-time students affiliated with the City University of New York, itself a massive public institution with twenty-five satellite campuses across the five boroughs, and adjacent to two New York City High Schools and a transitional correctional facility, all housed in former factory buildings, LPAC serves its student and neighborhood audiences with creative flair and fierce cultural pride. On March 12, 2015, the technical crew turned the lights down and projected the first film of what would become the yearly New York Forum of Amazigh Film or NYFAF.

Curated by the authors who are LaGuardia Community College professors, the idea for this festival emerged from an artistic and pedagogical project to showcase, engage in, and understand cultural diversity in the Muslim world through the arts. Called "Beyond Sacred: Unthinking Muslim Identity", this year-long multidisciplinary program of over fifty performances and community discussions was created to expand awareness and understanding of Muslim culture in post 9/11 New York City and to foster a complex understanding of Muslim identities. Presented at LPAC and performance and public spaces throughout the city, this ambitious cultural program also sought to open a dialogue between Muslim and non-Muslim communities and to challenge local notions of collective identity. As noted by City Councilman Peter Koo, representing the diverse Flushing, Queens neighborhood and one of several official sponsors of the program: "In an increasingly globalized society, it is important for people to learn as much as they can about the many different cultures on our planet. Anytime we can develop a better understanding of one another, barriers are removed, misperceptions are clarified, and the values that connect us as human beings move to the forefront".[7] As part of this effort, NYFAF chose to expose students and faculty to cinematic production from North Africa, a region of the world that remains much less familiar and visible to us in North America. As a pedagogical initiative, NYFAF sought to stage a way to "speak across difference", a key element of the college's core curriculum in global learning.

Right from the beginning, our location and audience began to shape NYFAF by inspiring us to seek a link between North Africa and the Americas. In our first edition in 2015, influenced by this link and the films we were able to find, we chose to focus on narratives by and about Indigenous peoples and the experience of migration. We called this two-day edition "New Voices in an Old World: The Berbers of North Africa" and developed a program that highlighted the multi-religious nature of Amazigh life and the painful and creative transformations that occur through emigration. These two themes were enhanced by the participation of Moroccan-French director Kamal Hachkar and Algerian-Italian novelist Amara Lakhous who came to share their work and engage with our audience. Due to the filmmakers' presence, the films we found and screened, and the location, we could sense a shift in curatorial perspective. Despite the diversity of their stated national and ethnic affiliations, the films led us from an Arab-Muslim dominant view of North Africa, in which Amazigh communities are viewed as a minority, to an Indigenous transnational Amazigh gaze. Likewise, our guests and audience led us to points of connection with Indigenous and immigrant experiences in North America. As a result, we changed the festival name to "The Berber/Amazigh Film Festival" the following year, and our second edition in 2016, titled "Breaking Borders and Bias: Human Rights, Minority Rights, and Artistic Expression", showcased films from across the Tamazgha, including the diaspora in Israel and Europe, increasing our commitment to a transnational representational space and a process of decolonizing this cinematic expression. Building on those first two years, NYFAF moved in 2017 to fully embrace its diverse Amazigh focus, taking on the name "The New York Forum of Amazigh Film". Our mission became clear: to celebrate and educate our audiences about "the history, culture, and language of Amazigh peoples across North Africa and in the diaspora" by disseminating and encouraging its emergent cinema (Boumlik and McNair 2017).

Throughout this period, the attempt to identify, locate, and screen Amazigh films proved to be a daunting yet productive facet of each edition, aided by scholars of North African film and new team-members. There are no nationally or internationally established film distribution networks for films focused on Amazigh ways of life. Indeed, when we started out, the very concept of an Amazigh film, a film that draws on Indigenous North African cultural modes and mores to represent everyday life and a relation to the land as well as to larger social, economic, and political forces such as colonialism and migration, was observable in discrete festival venues but not an established industry category. It was not part of scholarly studies of African cinema. Located at an international distance, in a place far from and unfamiliar with this cultural viewpoint and the problematics of its representation both artistically and logistically, and faced with no established distribution network, we sought access to films directly from filmmakers, producers, and other festivals, an arduous search that often encountered linguistic and technical obstacles.

We then took time to view and discuss the films we did acquire copies of with a team of invited speakers and collaborators including LaGuardia and CUNY faculty and scholars we met at an important conference held in Marrakesh, Morocco in the fall of 2016, "Transnational Moroccan Cinema", organized by film scholars Florence Martin, Will Higbee and Jamal Bahmad. By the 2017 edition, Yahya Laayouni and Soubeika (Wafa) Bahri joined NYFAF as core members, contributing hugely to our film search, web and program design, and social media outreach.

Our curatorial process was and remains collective, open to team-members and interns who join in the development of each edition. Together, we think through how and why the films we have found access to may represent or possess elements of an Amazigh worldview, and also how to present them to our diverse North American audience. We identify and trace thematic ties that enable us to introduce the films to our student audience and make connections for them, establishing the Little Theater as a site of pedagogical discovery, of intersemiotic and intercultural translation (Fig. 2).

The third edition, for example, which took place May 4–5, 2017, focused on the theme of "Transmission and Resistance: Towards a Pluralistic Society". It began with a discussion on the challenges faced by transnational North African Amazigh communities and their creative solutions. The guests were Bruce Maddy-Weitzman, Professor and Senior Research Fellow at Tel Aviv University, and Nabil Boudraa, Professor of French and Francophone Studies at Oregon State University. Films screened included *The Bicycle Owner* (short, Said Belli), *The Yellow House* (feature, Amor Hakkar), *Aman* (short, Estrella Monterrey), *They Were Promised the Sea* (feature, Kathy Wazana), *Amazigh Misr* (documentary, students of Ahram Canadian University of Media and Journalism/ ACU), *Addour* (feature, Ahmed Baidou), *King Rebel Proconsul* (short, Mohamed Megdoul), *Sin Eh* (short, Asem Gharsaa), and *Tomast N Teniri* (documentary, Solimane Salem Khalifa Hman). An important aspect of this edition was the participation of filmmaker Armando Ravelo (*Mah*, 2016) and female actor Estrella Monterrey (*Aman*, 2016) from the Canary Islands, where Amazigh language and cultural practices were obliterated by Spanish colonizers in the sixteenth and seventeenth centuries. It was nevertheless in the Canary Islands that the first Amazigh World Congress took place in 1997, gathering Amazigh activists from across the Tamazgha. Through the imaginative space of film, we were able to show how the historical presence of ancient Amazigh communities

Fig. 2 Poster for the 2019 5th edition of New York Forum of Amazigh Film (NYFAF) (Courtesy New York Forum of Amazigh Film)

serves as a site of contemporary cultural resistance and concern for environmental sustainability. Our largely Hispanic audience members were especially surprised and inspired by the Spanish-language connection.

In another example, the fifth edition (May 9–10, 2019) focused on "Exploring North African Identities" and introduced a competition for the best short film and a roundtable on Amazigh Cinema at Columbia University in collaboration with the Middle East Institute. Khadija El Mourabit, who plays the main character in the documentary *Khadija's Journey*, was a notable guest. The program included a musical performance and various other films: *The Mountain's Echo: The Voices of Amazigh Women* (documentary, Soufian Aaraichi), *Amazigh Wedding in the Anergui Valley* (documentary, Farida Benlyazid), *Defining Love, a Failed Attempt* (feature, Hakim Belabbas), *No* (short, Dimna Bounaylat),

Family in Exile (short, Fatima Matousse), *Afdis (The Hammer)* (short, Azro Magora), and *Lotos* (short, Slim Belguith). The program also included *Anâaq (Migrating)* (documentary, Mohamed Bouzia). The mix of female actors, filmmakers, and scholars who attended and participated in this 2019 edition planted a seed and we decided to initiate an editorial project of collected articles: *Amazigh Cinema: An Introduction to North African Indigenous Film*, co-edited by Lucy McNair and Yahya Laayouni and published by the University of Regina Press (2025), is the first book-length edited volume on Amazigh cinema in English.

5 Thematic Threads and Practical Solutions

Over time, watching films and deciding on which ones can find a place in a program developed around a communicable theme, NYFAF team members have noticed thematic threads weave through and between the filmmakers' visual worlds, pointing to common experiences. For example, a majority of these works represent a complex relationship to land, often establishing land and nature as a dramatic character or force. We also find that gender is spatially manifested through the use of environmental thresholds and the shift from a male to a female Indigenous gaze. In shorts, documentaries, and feature films, we found Amazigh filmmakers adept at addressing multiple spectatorships—local and diasporic Amazigh as well as national and global audiences—as they related histories of discrimination and bias or visually dramatized traditional oral and post-colonial literary narratives. Often through extreme wide shots, we noted how these films establish a character's experience of time, of space and duration, in testimony to Amazigh memory and resiliency.

We also note that the number of films set in the diaspora is increasing, which in turn impacts how we introduce notions of home and translocality. Though more recent films do not often make use of the diaspora to explicitly contrast the homeland and the foreign land, such contrasts subtly persist and are still indispensable parts of diasporic films that account for multiple sites of belonging. An example is the abovementioned *Khadija's Journey*, Tarik El Idrissi's documentary portrait of a Dutch-Moroccan woman in search of her grandmother's wisdom,[8] which illuminates the notion of polylocality, of living in two places simultaneously. Indeed, driven by a logic of flows, the world of Indigenous places (for example, the village home, the nearby city) is increasingly superseded by spaces characterized by circulation. Conversely, translocality implies multiple sites of identification (no longer a unique "Native place") and suggests that "home itself becomes complicated, its roots to a single locality multiplied to a network of localities" (Zhang 2010, 8). Translocality simultaneously designates three elements: places of attachment or identification (represented by ruins in the film *Azul*[9]); people whose physical or imaginary movements across scale connect disparate spaces and places (evident in the use of a video testimony in *The Yellow House*[10]); and technologies and modes of communication that facilitate such attachment, identification, movement, and connection (again evident in *Azul*) (Fig. 3).

Fig. 3 Poster for the 2023 8th edition of New York Forum of Amazigh Film (NYFAF) (Courtesy New York Forum of Amazigh Film)

These yearly journeys of discovery, of finding and "reading" films as Amazigh, due to our location and audience, have come to shape and enrich a pedagogical perspective on the films, making the festival itself an active location of layered cross-cultural encounter and exchange. Organized as a dual socio-cultural and pedagogical event (Vallejo and Peirano 2022, 231) where screenings are combined with Q&As, musical performances, course assignments, internships, and scholarly discussions, NYFAF acts as a pedagogical laboratory for dialogue across cultural differences through the means of cinema, a key element that continues to shape its programming. This laboratory actively encourages three types of community: a cultural community of filmmakers, musicians, producers, writers, and scholars; the "real" community of Queens, NY; and the large real and imagined community of Imazighen. To those we can add a virtual layer: during the COVID-19 pandemic in 2020 and 2022 we organized virtual editions centered on a chosen film and filmmaker, a practice we continued in combination with onsite screenings in 2023 and 2024. All three communities intersect at the yearly Forum to collectively address the Amazigh past and present, examining local, national, and diasporic or transnational contexts. Meeting in two spaces—on site in physical editions and online—and supportive of a new transnational Indigenous cinema, NYFAF facilitates the borderless flow of films and filmmakers and "allows the local to circulate globally" (Nichols 1994, 68).

Just like the Native Crossroads Film Festival documented by Severs, NYFAF's framework, combined with our college location, has specifically brought Indigenous filmmakers and both Indigenous and non-Indigenous audiences together. Indigenous audience members, often from Latin and South America, learn about the experiences, challenges, and viewpoints of Amazigh Indigenous communities while gaining insights into the potential of Indigenous cinema. Indeed, this unique pedagogical context actively responds to a broader reality of Indigenous film production and dissemination, namely the "contemporary transnational context of exchange and production" (Boumlik and McNair 2017). NYFAF has strategically used its curatorial role to make space for "audiences and cinematic practices otherwise marginalized or invisible within established film institutions and canons" (Rastegar 2012, 310). For example, when organizing the Short Film Competition for the festival in 2018, 2019, and 2024, we found ourselves receiving film submissions made specifically for dissemination at our festival by young filmmakers in the Maghreb and the North American diaspora.[11] By maintaining a broad understanding of what can constitute an Amazigh film and inviting and engaging with both established and novice filmmakers, NYFAF has benefitted from its location to gradually increase appreciation of Amazigh cinematic production as a category.

We see evidence of that commitment in our 9th edition which took place on April 18 and 19, 2024 when we returned to a two-day onsite program combined with a virtual format under the theme "Memory and Resilience". Taking place at LaGuardia and at Columbia University, with the support of the Middle East Institute, this edition showcased the work of French-Moroccan filmmaker Izza Génini who we were thrilled to invite, including a mini-retrospective of her films from the 1990s: *Vibrations in High Atlas*, (1993, 27 min), *Nuptials in Middle Atlas* (1993, 24 min), screened at LaGuardia, and *Aita* (France/Morocco, 1988, 27 min) and *The Citron, Fruit of Splendor* (France/Morocco, 1998, 30 min) screened and discussed at Columbia University's Middle East Institute. A self-taught, Jewish Moroccan-French documentary filmmaker, Génini's short personal testimonies of Amazigh rituals, musical traditions, and women's ways of knowing trace a relationship between the sacred and the profane, the spiritual and the mundane, with a steady eye on the link between people and natural forces. A range of other shorts and features shed light on the ways Amazigh individuals and communities resist religious fundamentalism that discriminates against Amazigh cultural practices (*The Song of Sin* by Khalid Maddour, Morocco, 2022, 14 min), memorialize collective trauma (*Bloody Memories* by Mourad Bouamrane, Algeria, 2024, 37 min) and beloved literary figures (*Fouroulou* by Ali Berkennou, Algeria, 2023, 93 min), and represent the choice some young Amazigh people face between the desert and exile (*The House Is On Fire, Might As Well Get Warm* by Mouloud Ouyahia, France, 2023, 43 min).

6   Conclusion

To conclude, a review of our nine festival editions reveals a critical self-reflection: there is no clear line of demarcation between what is an Amazigh film and what is not. The films themselves compel us to recognize this indistinction. Nor is our attempt to establish this genre through thematic formats that link North African Indigenous film with North American experiences without incoherence at times, dictated as the editions are by the quality or number of films received. NYFAF reflects and works with the reality of the moment as the #MeToo movement and the COVID-19 pandemic showed us, further influencing the festival's structure. Yet these nine years have taught us that each film creates a "small planet" in the style of Elinor Fuch's (2004) dramaturgical model, showcasing diversity within a continuum of identity, and reinforcing NYFAF's commitment to increasing visibility for Amazigh people in their complexity through film.

Without doubt however, the cultural specificity and the location and audience of an Indigenous film festival, in this case an African Indigenous festival, can build a dialogic rapport between filmmakers, scholars, and audience members which can elevate and pass onward an emergent cinema. Through yearly journeys of discovery and thematically developed pedagogical tools, NYFAF has moved from a more traditional gaze on the region's diverse film production to a multidirectional, decolonizing process of screening, discussing, and inspiring, joining in effect the filmmakers' efforts to establish what Pamela Wilson has called "Indigenous representational sovereignty" (2016, 97) of North African groups. Offering a new example of Nigel Reading's "fusion format" of exhibition and display as well (cited in Petty and Benbouazza 2019, 60), NYFAF seeks to be a festival that gives back by passing forward, operating within the space of post- and/or de-colonial memory. In this way, NYFAF contributes to the framing of the discussion around a crucial question: can contemporary African Film Festivals create a location for public history and the rebuilding of collective memory?

Competing Interests Research for this chapter draws on research work developed through Social Sciences and Humanities Research Council of Canada Partnership Development Grant #890–2020-0102.

Notes

1. Historically referred to as "Berber", Amazigh (singular) or Imazighen (plural) are terms that refer to Indigenous inhabitants of the Tamazgha, a geographical neologism established by Amazigh groups in the late 20th c based on historical records of habitation. This area stretches from the Canary Islands in the Atlantic Ocean across Morocco, Algeria, Tunisia, Libya, and Egypt, and south to

Mauritania, Mali and Niger, including Imazighen living today in the diaspora in Europe, Canada and the US.
2. Amazighity is a term connecting Amazigh cultural expression, transnational identity, and Indigenous consciousness. See El Guabli (2021).
3. Examples of Indigenous film festivals: The Dreamspeakers Festival in Edmonton, Alberta, Canada; The imagineNATIVE Film and Media Arts Festival in Toronto, Canada; The Terres en Vue/Land In Sights First People Festival in Montreal, Canada; The Native American Film and Video Festival in New York City; The American Indian Film Festival in San Francisco (1975); The Sundance Institute's Native and Indigenous Institute at the Sundance Film Festival; The Message Sticks Festival in Australia; National Geographic's All Roads Festival; The Wairoa Maori Film Festival in New Zealand.
4. Among the well-established film festivals, we could cite Congreso Latinoamericano de Antropología (ALA) and Reunión de Antropología del Mercosur (RAM) and Encuentro de Antropología Audiovisual organized by the Red Mexicana de Antropologia Visual (REMAV).
5. Efforts of inter-festival regional exchanges can be illustrated by the Argentinian Muestra Nacional de Cine y Video Documental Antropológico y Social (DocAnt, National Showcase of Anthropological and Social Documentary Film and Video) and the INAPL, the National Institute of Anthropology and Latin American Thought.
6. AMREC: L'Association marocaine de recherche et d'échange culturel.
7. "LaGuardia Community College Launches "Beyond Sacred" Showcasing Muslim Culture, Identity In Post-9/11 New York City" (September 9, 2014).
   https://www1.cuny.edu/mu/forum/2014/09/09/laguardia-community-college-launches-beyond-sacred-showcasing-muslim-culture-identity-in-post-911-new-york-city/.
8. *Khadija's Journey* by Tarik El Idrissi 2017 depicts Khadija, a young woman born in Amsterdam. Hindered by personal circumstances, she returns to her village to reconcile with her past, origins, and reconnect with her idol: her paternal grandmother, Mamma Allal.

9. *Azul* by Wassim Korbi, Tunisia, 2013, is a documentary offering insights into the director's personal journey to his father's village, situated in an area where the culture of the *Imazighen* is struggling to survive in the last bastions of *Amazigh* land. As Korbi explores the region and speaks with local Imazighen, the lived experiences of their daily lives are explored.
10. This feature film is about the family of Mouloud, a peasant in the Algerian mountains who learns of the tragic loss of their soldier son who has been killed in an ambush. Mouloud sets off to retrieve his son's body. When he returns home, he finds his wife Fatima has closed herself off into a world of suffering. A video is found among their son's belongings that changes the course of events. The film explores themes of grief and loss.
11. Examples of short films submitted exclusively to NYFAF are: *Tinghir* by Aisha Jabour (Morocco, 2014, 7 min), a documentary observation of the filmmaker's family home in Tinghir, Morocco, on the days following the funeral of her cousin; *Thasakoorth* by Miriem Sadoun (USA, 2017, 6 min), a short about the legend of Kahina who lives a quiet life in a cabin on the edge of the forest, also recalling a series of events that led to the death of her mother; *Barbary Fig* by Bianca Boragi (Short, USA/Algeria, 2017, 18 min), a short about Ghalia's daughter who asks to travel to Great Kabylia in Algeria to visit the grave of her grandmother. Ghalia rejects the idea and starts to remember fragments of her difficult life growing up during the Algerian War of Independence (1954-1962); *Pulsation* by Iskandar Tlili (Tunisia, 2017, 3 min silent), a short about old age, female power and powerlessness, the ancient past and the speeding present; *The Mountain's Echo: The Voices of Amazigh Women* by Soufian Aaraichi, (documentary, 2015, 16 min); *Tekrouna* (Tunisia, 2015); and *Afdis (The Hammer)* (Libya, 2017).

References

Boumlik, Habiba, and Lucy R. McNair. 2017. Looking for Amazigh Cinema—Developing The New York Forum of Amazigh Film. *Transnational Moroccan Cinema*. https://moroccancinema.exeter.ac.uk/en/habiba-boumlik-and-lucy-mcnair-summary/. Accessed 15 August 2024.

Carter, Sandra Gayle. 2001. Moroccan Berberity, Representational Power and Identity in Video Films. *International Communication Gazette* 63 (2–3): 241–262.

Devaux Yahi, Frédérique. 2017. Films berbères et identités. *Nouveaux cahiers de Marge* 1. https://publications-prairial.fr/marge/index.php?id=187. Accessed 20 July 2024.

El Guabli, Brahim. 2021. My Amazigh Indigeneity (The Bifurcated Roots of a Native Moroccan). *The Markaz Review*, September 15.

El Idrissi, Tarik. 2017. (Director). *Khadija's Journey*, (2017) [film].

Film Festival Research. http://www.filmfestivalresearch.org/index.php/ffrn-bibliography/1-film-festivals-the-long-view/.

Fuchs, Elinor. 2004. EF's Visit to a Small Planet: Some Questions to Ask a Play. *Theater* 34 (2): 5–9. https://doi.org/10.1215/01610775-34-2-5.

Graham, Laura R., and H. Glenn Penny, eds. 2014. *Performing Indigeneity: Global Histories and Contemporary Experiences*. UNP—Nebraska. ProQuest Ebook Central. http://ebookcentral.proquest.com/lib/lagcc-ebooks/detail.action?docID=1813560.

McNair, Lucy R., and Yahya Laayouni. 2021. Amazigh Cinema and the New York Forum of Amazigh Film. *Jadaliyya*, November. https://www.jadaliyya.com/Details/43443.

Merolla, Daniela. 2020. Les films en amazigh "Grand Ecran" et "Amazighwood." *Études Et Documents Berbères* 1 (1): 67–89.

Merolla, Daniella, Kamal Nait Zerad, and Amer Amezianne, eds. 2019. *Les cinémas berbères. De la méconnaissance aux festivals internationaux*. Paris: Karthala.

Nichols, Bill. 1994. Global Image Consumption in the Age of Late Capitalism. *East-West Film Journal* 8 (1): 68–85.

Papadimitriou, Lydia, and Jeffrey Ruoff. 2016. Film Festivals: Origins and Trajectories. *New Review of Film and Television Studies* 14 (1): 1–4. https://doi.org/10.1080/17400309.2015.1106686.

Peirano, Maria Paz. 2017. Ethnographic and Indigenous Film Festivals in Latin America: Constructing Networks of Film Circulation. In *Film Festivals and Anthropology*, ed. Aida Vallejo and Maria Paz Peirano, 73–88. Newcastle upon Tyne: Cambridge Scholars Publishing.

Petty, Sheila, and Brahim Benbouazza. 2019. Trans-Indigenous Aesthetics and Practices in Moroccan Amazigh Film and Video. *Expressions Maghrébines* 18 (1): 47–62.

Rastegar, Roya. 2012. Difference, Aesthetics and the Curatorial Crisis of Film Festivals. *Screen* 53 (3): 310–317. https://doi.org/10.1093/screen/hjs022.

Severs, Caitlin. 2019. *Visual Sovereignty and Indigenous Film Festivals: A Case Study on The Native Crossroads Film Festival*, Master's Thesis, University of Oklahoma. OU Theses. https://hdl.handle.net/11244/319644.

Soussi, Houssine. 2019. Amazigh International Film Festivals and the Promotion of Amazigh Cinema. Conference: The Annual Kurultai of the Endangered Cultural Heritage. AKECH 2019, Constanţa, Romania.

Turan, Kenneth. 2002. *Sundance to Sarajevo: Film Festivals and the World They Made*. Berkeley: University of California Press.

Vallejo, Aida, and Maria Paz Peirano. 2022. Conceptualising Festival Ecosystems: Insights from the Ethnographic Film Festival Subcircuit. *Studies in European Cinema* 19 (3): 231–251. https://doi.org/10.1080/17411548.2022.2103930.

Wilson, Pamela. 2016. Indigenous Documentary Media. In *Contemporary Documentary*, ed. Daniel Marcus and Selmin Kara, 87–104. Oxon and New York: Routledge.

Wong, Cindy Hing-Yuk. 2011. *Film Festivals: Culture, People, and Power on the Global Screen*. New Brunswick, NJ: Rutgers University Press.

Zhang, Y. 2010. *Cinema, Space, and Polylocality in a Globalizing China*. Honolulu: University of Hawai'i Press.

Open Access This chapter is licensed under the terms of the Creative Commons Attribution 4.0 International License (http://creativecommons.org/licenses/by/4.0/), which permits use, sharing, adaptation, distribution and reproduction in any medium or format, as long as you give appropriate credit to the original author(s) and the source, provide a link to the Creative Commons license and indicate if changes were made.

The images or other third party material in this chapter are included in the chapter's Creative Commons license, unless indicated otherwise in a credit line to the material. If material is not included in the chapter's Creative Commons license and your intended use is not permitted by statutory regulation or exceeds the permitted use, you will need to obtain permission directly from the copyright holder.

CHAPTER 5

Virtualization of the New York Forum of Amazigh Film (NYFAF) During and Post-COVID-19: The Scramble "To Remain the Same"

Soubeika Bahri

Abstract Amid the COVID-19 global pandemic and just like many film festivals around the world, the New York Forum of Amazigh Film (NYFAF) also had to pivot to online and hybrid formats. The virtualization of the film event primarily meant transforming its relationship with the filmmakers and audience and changing the ways its organizers function between each edition while considering the pedagogical and transnational aspects of the forum. Drawing loosely on de Valck

---

De Valck, Marijke, and Antoine Damiens. 2023. *Rethinking Film Festivals in the Pandemic Era and After*. Cham: Springer International Publishing.

S. Bahri (✉)
Applied Linguistics Department, University of Massachusetts, Boston, MA, USA
e-mail: Soubeika.Bahri@umb.edu

© The Author(s) 2025
S. Petty (ed.), *African Film Festivals and Transnational Flows of Living Cultural Heritage*, Framing Film Festivals,
https://doi.org/10.1007/978-3-031-88590-7_5

and Damiens' concept of "scrambled to remain the same", this chapter examines the online and hybrid transitioning as new strategies and opportunities adopted by the NYFAF organizers to pivot and re-imagine a future look for this film forum with this new approach. The chapter argues for a different understanding of the virtualization approach and points to the importance of a reflection on the expressions of resilience, disruption, and place, particularly in the context of small "genre" film festivals.

Keywords NYFAF · Amazigh film · Online · Hybrid · COVID-19 pandemic

1 Introduction

The impact of the COVID-19 pandemic was felt across all industries and sectors, including film festivals. The New York Forum of Amazigh Film (NYFAF), like many others, had to quickly adapt to the changing circumstances in 2020. As the crisis unfolded, it became clear that fundamental transformations and structural changes were essential. The transition to a virtual format required new decisions and planning in terms of film exhibition, audience engagement, and communal access. Operating completely outside a bricks and mortar theater involved a redesign of the event setup and a renegotiation of new infrastructures and technical support (Loist 2023, 18). By moving to a digital platform, a new format was adopted in NYFAF sixth, seventh, and eight editions pushing the festival to scramble "to remain the same" (de Valck and Damiens 2023, 219). The idea of scrambling to remain the same draws on the analogy of the formula "habit + crisis = update", which was proposed by new media scholar Wendy Hui Kyong Chun (2016). In the case of film festivals, the formula refers to the attempt to simulate onsite film festival encounters during times of crisis. As for NYFAF, the scrambling updates forced the editions of the years 2020, 2022, and 2023 to be organized in at least two different formats (online and hybrid), while the question of its survival beyond its usual "spatio-temporal boundaries" (de Valck and Damiens 2023, 3) became a central concern.

This concern relates to Burgess and Stevens' (2023, 61) observation regarding the transformation of festivals' networking publics into networked publics, and how it is crucial to reconsider the performative aspects of the festival experience and value creation in the context of the virtual world. In the words of Skadi Loist, "the pandemic acted mostly as a magnifying glass and accelerator for existing structures and mechanisms.....trends that had already started to appear due to the digitalization of industry and entertainment consumption" (2023, 17–18). In this chapter I will examine how NYFAF faced the COVID-19 challenges, and the strategies employed to create a blend of online and onsite platforms in productive ways during the past four years. Most significantly, I will probe how this film forum has managed to maintain its identity and mission despite the numerous uncertainties the pandemic and post-pandemic era brought, particularly for local, small "genre", or Indigenous film festivals, such as NYFAF.

2   NYFAF in Context

The New York Forum of Amazigh Film (NYFAF) is an annual event that takes place in the spring, typically in April or May, at the LaGuardia Performing Arts Center's Little Theater in the borough of Queens in New York City. Co-founded by Drs. Habiba Boumlik and Lucy McNair, the event aims to explore global issues through the lens of Indigenous North African, sub-Saharan, and diasporic cinema. Its mission is to promote Amazigh cultural expression(s) and foster connections between Tamazgha[1] and North American audiences. NYFAF provides free access to all screenings and is open to the general public, but students make up much of its audience. This is because the venue where it takes place is an educational institution—La Guardia Community College. Like most small and identity-based festivals around the world, NYFAF relies heavily on volunteers and organizers who are committed to the event out of love, academic interest, and in this case, support for Amazigh culture and identity. In a personal interview with Habiba Boumlik, festival co-curator, she commented:

> Our team reflects the resilience of the Amazigh people. Our impact may be modest, our means are limited, but our efforts will sustain the obstacles. We are all volunteers; we grow through this endeavor; it enriches us and I would like to honor my large Amazigh community, long silenced, by providing some visibility to its cinematic creation and knowledge. (Boumlik, May 31, 2024)

The event is named "forum" instead of "festival" to create an open platform for various artistic expressions, new talents, and emerging voices. The choice of "forum" stems from being the closest translation to *Asmagraw* in the Amazigh dialect of Southern Morocco, Tashalhyt. This term inspired the curators during their search for an Amazigh expression that could frame the objectives of this project. According to McNair and Boumlik, *Asmagraw* is a forum that aims to reclaim tolerance in a world that is becoming increasingly intolerant, especially for marginalized, minority, and subaltern identities associated with the Imazighen (plural of Amazigh) (Boumlik and McNair 2017).

What makes NYFAF unique is its strong focus on pedagogy. As McNair and Laayouni write, NYFAF is meant to "model an educational practice of approaching cultural and linguistic diversity through an indigenous, transnational cinema by means of screenings and discussions for a diverse audience" (2021, 2). NYFAF organizers integrate the forum's themes and program content into courses and seminars they teach during the spring semesters. Correspondingly, classroom discussions and readings are informed by the forum's programming and students' participation in the event either as audience or Q&A moderators. The educational dimension of NYFAF is also shaped through assignments based on showcased films during the forum and relatable readings. NYFAF considers pedagogy one of its defining principles and commitment to cultivate and nurture discussions and possibilities of transformative learning, thinking, and acting. In this sense, NYFAF has become a site where cinematic and media production intersects with pedagogical praxis leading to lively exchanges.

Another fundamental and defining feature of NYFAF is its transnational perspective. In the words of McNair and Laayouni (2021) in their Jadaliyya[2] article: "Amazigh Cinema and the New York Forum of Amazigh Film (NYFAF)":

> Our approach actively seeks to shape a practice of transnational exchange that can nourish this space of intersemiotic translation of Amazigh life and "translate" it further to a larger audience. Rejecting any folkloric or essentialist perspective, we showcase all possible formats - short films, documentaries and feature films produced for television and cinemas, including first films by diasporic filmmakers. We accept films about the whole width of the Tamazgha [...] to this geographical space, we add the European and North American diasporas. As we develop each edition, we stay

attentive to major issues that emerge: the passage from oral to cinematographic narration, the multiple avenues of reception by the public, social conflicts around gender, work, and immigration, the evolution of identities stretched between home and diasporic locations, and the basics of how to get films made and distributed. (McNair and Laayouni 2021)

The pandemic disruption created a moment of confusion over the fate of the forum's spatio-temporality, audience, and above all its transnational and pedagogical goals. Like many specialized and localized film festivals, NYFAF organizers scrambled over different imaginations of its future during the pandemic, contemplating possibilities of postponing or cancelling the festival, transitioning to a fully online mode, and/ or moving to a temporary hybrid format. To understand how NYFAF managed the alternative solutions and formats, it is important to situate each of them within analytical frameworks of film festivals in times of crisis, change, and disruption.

3 Film Festivals in Times of Crisis: Framework

As film festivals experimented with different options for their survival and sustainability, the uncertainty of the unprecedented circumstances of the global pandemic forced many of them throughout Africa, Europe, Asia, North America, and Australia to halt or cancel their events completely, as was the case of many US Latinx Film Festivals such as San Diego Latino Film Festival (SDLFF) and South by Southwest (SXSW). De Valck accurately points out that these festivals understood that "when the purpose of a film festival surpasses the screening of films, the void that is left by the cancellation of physical events cannot be filled with online offerings exclusively" (2020, 129). Founded through the private initiatives of enthusiastic filmmakers and/or cultural managers who apply to local funds and often struggle with audience attendance and lack of media coverage or strong marketing support, the festivals endured additional drastic effects during the disruptive times of the global health crisis (Peirano and Ramírez 2023, 130). Hence, attempts to make last minute updates by moving from physical, in-person projection to the digital world, required different resources of mobility and accessibility that not every festival has the same capacity to fulfill. Planning for a festival is time-consuming. And yet ensuring its continuity remains a major point of concern that pushed festival organizers to bring some version of the festival experience to the audience or think of a strategy that would keep it going. This is perhaps why, according to the Film Festival Alliance (FFA) survey of film organizers, only 2% of responding film festival organizers reported that they cancelled all of their 2020 events and 73% adopted an online/virtual version in the same year, while 14% planned for an online event and 6% chose to keep the in-person format (Davis 2021, 11).

Following March 2020, however, most festivals around the world were forced into adopting new formats and taking new measures. The decision to cancel is one type of response that affected even large film festivals, such as Seattle International Film Festival (SIFF). According to Davis (2021, 14–15), this 45-year-old event was planning to showcase their usual 250 features, host their 175,000+ attendees, and turn Seattle springtime into its usual cultural festive season before they realized that they could neither digitalize the program nor postpone it to summer, when the pandemic hit. Since the cancellation of one of the larger, if not the largest, festivals in the United States was inevitable, it is expected that some types of small, regional, and/or Indigenous festivals would face the same fate during this time of adversity and decisions for rescheduling new dates were contingent upon not only local circumstances but also the changing ecosystem for these small cinema events (Loist 2023, 20). Among these were Indigenous film festivals, such as Cine Las Americas International Film Festival (part of a small community-oriented identity-based group of film festivals dedicated to improving the representation of the Latinx and Indigenous communities that takes place in Austin Texas) (Cheyroux 2023, 49) and the RED, *Red de Festivales y Muestras de Cine de Chile y los Pueblos Originarios* (Network of Chilean and Indigenous Film Festivals) (Peirano and Ramírez 2023, 129). Indeed, the cancellation of these categories of festivals impacted not only the geographic organization of the physical festival experience that has long revolved around the importance of the "big screen" cinema experience and the bonding and networking objectives (Smits 2023, 313), but also their role as cultural entities that promote better representation of minorities and Indigenous groups, and counterbalance other content found on mainstream platforms (Cheyroux 2023, 49).

While many of those small and local festivals managed to re-emerge beginning in June 2020, they were forced to move their schedules and reshape their programs and activities; reorganize their teams; reconfigure their alliances; and redirect remaining funds from 2019 to different expenses in 2020 (Peirano and Ramírez 2023, 133). De Valck and

Damiens argue that "online festivals cannot be thought of as a measure that could be implemented uniformly without any consideration of local contexts" (2023, 5). They add that the virtual and de-territorialized space of the internet is necessarily inflected by very local concerns over access, infrastructure, and cultural habits (2023, 4). However, the benefits of online festival streaming include increased accessibility of films to potentially larger and more diverse audiences and flexibility in terms of the space, time and choice of viewing. According to data gathered by organizers of Cleveland International Film Festival (CIFF), a region-focused film festival that transitioned online, the festival had 70% of its program viewed, more revenues gained, a wider audience reached than in previous years, and over 80% of the surveyed audience reported having a great or fantastic experience, which made the organizers decide to continue using the online version even once the pandemic ended (Davis 2021, 21–22). Smits argues for the online format as part of the continuing process of cultural change in the current increasingly online society rather than as a form of disruption with "disturbing and upsetting influence" (2023, 311). Brunow contends that the online format can nurture a sense of togetherness and collective experience through "the interplay of multimodal forms of engagement: via social media, an online platform, via chat entries, tweets, gestures, participation in live discussions, or streaming oneself watching the livestream" (2020, 340). She adds that shifting to an online cinema platform that can guarantee the flexibility and spatial relocation anytime and anywhere resonates with the increasingly transnational, or at least trans-local, public of online film festivals (Brunow 2020, 339–347).

The advantages of the online format, however, were not necessarily equally accessible for audiences who were faced with a mix of technological, personal, and cultural barriers (Damiens and de Valck 2023, 9). In the same vein, cinema critics and film professionals expressed anxiety over the digital shift of film festivals for fear it would not sufficiently simulate the liveness and co-presence that make up the festival atmosphere (Loist 2023; Kohn and Thompson 2021). In a *TFCBlog* published by Jeffrey Winter in May 2020 under the title "A Way of Life in Peril: Film Festival Distribution in the Age of COVID-19", he characterized the online model shift as a simple decision lacking innovation. Furthermore, while discussions and debates can still take place via the Zoom chat affordance, they often take the form of emotional communication or brief comments and questions that are more concerned with making one's presence known to others than with the exchange of novel ideas (Vail et al. 2023, 82). More importantly, as audiences are no longer confined to a screening calendar or physical theater but can view the films over longer streaming periods, risks of pirating the films or running into unauthorized use of materials through the showcased films are more likely to arise. These concerns led many festivals, such as Vues d'Afrique in Canada, to opt for geo-blocking of viewers to reduce risks of copyright infringement and extra-costs of the digital distribution.

By 2021, several film festivals around the world shifted to a hybrid format, combining in-person events with online screenings. This move towards hybridity is seen as a step towards reimagining what a twenty-first century film festival could be. However, concerns have been raised about the financial and logistical challenges, particularly regarding less well-funded festivals. Despite these concerns, there is a growing recognition that the changes brought about by COVID-19 are likely to have a lasting impact (Kredell 2023, 44). In support of this assumption, Vail et al. (2023, 86) note:

> It's important to understand the diversity of online film festival audiences, especially as festivals continue to evolve and incorporate both online and in-person film screenings. This understanding will help audiences navigate hybrid festival programs and decide where and how they want to watch films. Film festivals now have the choice to cater to new types of digital audiences, traditional in-person audiences, or take a blended approach that combines both online and in-person experiences.

Community-oriented or identity focused film festivals are illustrative of successful examples of festivals which opted for the hybrid format during the pandemic. The Outfest Los Angeles Film Festival, centered around empowering and showcasing the works and artists of the LGBTQIA+ community, is an example of a festival that presented a hybrid version and garnered good satisfaction and positive reception from the community (Davis 2021, 38). The success of the hybrid format encouraged the festival's organizers to maintain it longer than originally anticipated while they seem to have remained mindful of the importance of retaining the in-person traditional format. In what follows, the focus will be on the case of NYFAF. Since COVID-19, the range of options for this forum include: returning to in-person events; remaining exclusively online; or adopting a hybrid approach.

4 Methodology

This chapter focuses on the case study of NYFAF's strategies for survival during the COVID-19 pandemic, that serve as a model of cultural resilience and innovation for other small, local, or Indigenous events facing adversity. The analysis employs a qualitative approach that includes interviews with the curators of the forum, as well as audience reactions and feedback collected through NYFAF Q&A sessions, informal conversations with the author during the onsite or online versions, social media comments, and the chat feature used in Zoom during the virtual editions. The interviews were conducted using a structured set of questions throughout May 2024. Additional data was collected through an online ethnography note-taking format, which involved tracking interactions and comments within digital spaces, primarily Zoom, Facebook, and emails sent to the organizers after each edition discussed in this chapter. Each note entry was organized by date, platform, and participant. The next step involved employing a content analysis thematic approach to categorize the entries and interview responses into four major themes: comments about the in-person versus virtual formats of NYFAF, comments about the organizers of the NYFAF, comments about the audience, and comments about the films and program lineups. The data set also encompassed an array of program brochures, flyers, and engaging content from the NYFAF website. Delving into this rich collection proved instrumental in uncovering the diverse strategies and innovative tactics that were implemented to ensure the forum's ongoing operation throughout the challenges posed by the pandemic and beyond.

5 NYFAF: Navigating Strategies of Survival

Following the declaration of a global COVID-19 pandemic by the World Health Organization on March 11, 2020, many public and private institutions worldwide, including those in New York City, had to close and transition to remote operations. The City University of New York (CUNY) was among the institutions affected by these changes. CUNY,[3] with approximately 250,000 students and 45,000 faculty across twenty-five campuses, had to transition to a digital format for teaching and learning and university administrative operations. This transition posed challenges and raised concerns about equity and access for the most vulnerable students, faculty, and staff. LaGuardia Community College, as part of CUNY, also had to abide by lockdown rules.

On the LaGuardia Community College website,[4] The LaGuardia Performing Arts Center (LPAC) is introduced as an internationally recognized producer and presenter of new live dance, theater, music, and multidisciplinary programming that reflects the dynamic community of Queens and the surrounding New York City. LPAC is located within LaGuardia Community College, a cultural crossroads that provides an educational and artistic home to New York City's most diverse community. Each year, nearly 20,000 individuals attend performances by international artists in the venue's 740-seat state-of-the-art proscenium theater (Main Stage) and 200-seat multipurpose theater (Little Theater). NYFAF has been in the Little Theater since its inception in 2015.

The New York Forum of Amazigh Film (NYFAF) is typically held during the spring semester in April or May. By the time the lockdown was ordered in March 2020, the festival organizers had already finalized the film lineup and program. The forum was scheduled for two days on May 21 and May 22, focusing on the theme of *transgenerational relationships*. The first day was planned to take place at the Little Theater while the second day was set to be at the Maysles Documentary Center in Harlem, New York City. NYFAF had always sought collaboration with other local venues in addition to LPAC to expand its audience reach and fulfill its educational objectives. For example, part of the 2018 edition took place at The Middle East Institute at Columbia University. Moving the forum online posed layers of challenges as it meant not only giving up potential collaboration with the Harlem venue but also changing the entire program and adapting to new screening requirements, which added to the already stressful situation for the organizers who are professors and who had to also struggle with the sudden shift to online teaching in their classrooms.

Committed to keeping the event running and to continue bringing Amazigh cinema to the diasporic world, the organizers considered the online transition an opportunity to use a technological platform to reach out to national and international audiences despite all the challenges and restrictions that came with this choice. Adapting to the new online mode of presentation, NYFAF began by changing the theme from *transgenerational relationships* to *streaming with a purpose*. The choice of this theme was inspired by a desire to capture the vulnerability and resilience of the forum during a time of adversity. Reducing the program to one film was another tough decision and came because of the uncertainty of the situation and unfamiliarity with the new parameters of online screenings. The selected film was *Islam of My Childhood* (2019, Canada) by Kabyle-Algerian-Canadian filmmaker Nadia Zouaoui. The film was chosen for a couple of reasons. First, it was related to the filmmaker's acceptance of the forum's invitation to participate in the film discussion and Q&A session. Second, the film's narrative focuses on the filmmaker's return to her home country to search for the peaceful Islam she knew growing up. During this road movie, Zouaoui travels around Algeria and uncovers memories of people traumatized by Algeria's "Black Decade", a period during the 1990s of extreme difficulties and turbulent events caused by Islamist terrorists bent on transforming Algeria into a sharia-based Islamic State. The film's narrative of navigating turbulent times and building resilience resonated with the challenges faced by the forum in adapting to the crisis and fragility caused by the pandemic.

The next challenge for the festival organizers was the logistics of arranging a platform to host the film and determining how to screen it. It was decided to have the film available for password-protected screening on the theater website for forty-eight hours from May 26 through 28 and then hold a Zoom panel discussion and Q&A with the filmmaker on May 29. The panel discussion was equally energetic and enriching as it unpacked the role of memory in trauma healing, the complex ways in which gender shapes war memories, the importance of un-silencing a dark past, and the need to find new methods for understanding history linked to religious or political violence. In addition to Nadia Zouaoui, the discussion featured a fair number of scholars and students from different colleges and universities around the United States, Canada, and North Africa. In a follow-up conversation about the first online experience, the organizers found it quite enthralling as it offered an unprecedented opportunity for NYFAF to make global connections and reach an audience beyond New York City.

The organizers decided to launch a second online part of the 6th edition in the fall, on November 20, 2020. Still under the theme *streaming with a purpose* and in alignment with the fragility and resilience of the Kabyle people during the Black Decade as depicted in *Islam of My Childhood*, the NYFAF team selected *Papicha* (2019, Algeria/France/Belgium/Qatar) by the French/Kabyle filmmaker Mounia Meddour. *Papicha*, which means "rebel girl", is the story of Nedjma, a young clothing designer in Algeria who organizes a fashion show as an act of rebellion against a repressive society and in memory of her sister who was tragically murdered.

During the discussion, scholars such as Nabil Boudraa, Yahya Laayouni, Kawtare Bihya, and Fazia Aïtel provided context about the Black Decade. Additionally, Samira Negrouche, an Algerian poet recited her poem "Minus One" (2020) in French, which was interpreted into English by Marilyn Hacker. Amira Hilda Douaouda, who plays Samira in the film, was also present during the Q&A and shared her insights and experiences of the film production and reception, particularly focusing on the 2019 protests in Algeria, known as the *Revolution of Smiles* or the *Hirak Movement*.[5] The discussion evolved around several thought-provoking topics such as Islam, colonization, a multilingual society, women's rights, and the control of public spaces like universities; and the chat was lively and enthusiastic, featuring participants and students from as far away as Pakistan and Dominican Republic. The unexpected positive reaction led Habiba Boumlik to declare in response to an interview question by the author:

> I was very concerned about the audience response to our virtual edition. However, thanks to the plethora of events and festivals offered virtually during the pandemic, the turnout was not bad at all. We actually gained some people who were able to join us for the first time, from parts of NY and the world. (Boumlik, May 31, 2024)

By all accounts, both versions of the online experience were very successful allowing NYFAF to embrace, in the words of Karlekar, "a positive, even utopian vision of the virtual global village" (2023, 242). The online experiences allowed the introduction of novel spaces and tools for connections and communications with audiences. Using Zoom or the Facebook account which streamed the 6th and 7th online editions Live, combined with written feedback and in-meeting reactions emoji to signal presence or appreciation via likes, hearts, and clapping hands added more interactions and enabled more dynamic panel discussions.

In 2021, the pandemic persisted, with periodic restrictions on people's mobility, including lockdowns, curfews, limited opening hours for movie theaters, and capacity controls. These COVID-related effects and restrictions had varying impacts on the film, media, and cultural sectors at different levels. As noted by de Valck and Damiens, "the crisis does not necessarily impact every festival at the same time or to the same extent"

(2023, 8). To comprehend the effects of COVID-19 on the film festival operational system and on the film, media, and cultural sectors as a whole, it is useful to consider local contexts and individual responses. In the case of NYFAF, the pandemic significantly reduced the number of film submissions. Many filmmakers chose to wait out the pandemic. Additionally, the pandemic imposed a significant paradigm shift in education from traditional methods to digital teaching. NYFAF organizers, like most educators in the world, had to face unprecedented pressure to upgrade their digital literacy, accommodate lack of access to technology and the internet, especially for students from lower socioeconomic backgrounds, and find ways that help combat Zoom fatigue. Since there was so much to understand and update to reduce teachers' burnout and accommodate students' cognitive, emotional, and social transitioning to new learning platforms, a need for a break from extra-curricular, cultural, or festival activity seemed critical.

Considering these challenges, NYFAF had to decide how to proceed for its 7th edition. Eventually, the event was canceled in 2021 and the 7th edition was postponed to 2022. The organizers used this moment of rupture to rethink the forum's dependencies on spatial positioning, the changing ecosystem, and local and individual circumstances to find alternative solutions that maintain the "eventness" of any film festival (Olibet and Thain 2023, 160).

The pandemic enabled NYFAF to engage not only wider, but also more diverse audiences. It allowed more filmmakers, distributors, and actors who might not previously be able to travel for visa issues or health crisis traveling bans to participate in the online panel discussions and Q&A sessions. In this way, "it was able to reach a more variegated audience across geographical boundaries" (Karlekar 2023, 243). In answering interview questions to write this chapter, Habiba Boumlik, notes:

> I think the shift has proven to be positive given that we are still able to draw on viewers and participants from various parts of the world. The online edition seems to be very convenient for people who cannot attend the in-person edition, and it leads to good interactions through chats and Q&A. The panel discussion enables scholarly film discussions that benefit a larger audience. (Boumlik, May 31, 2024)

After a one-year break, NYFAF chose to return to the online mode from April 26 through May 3, 2022. Unlike many film festivals which returned to some form of pre-COVID in-person operations, NYFAF maintained its online mode while continuing with its *streaming with a purpose* theme. The decision was mainly motivated by a desire to maintain the national and transnational audience reach that was achieved through the digitalization of the event. Therefore, NYFAF wanted to continue benefiting from what Burgess and Stevens referred to as "the elasticity and potential porousness of the festival's spatial boundaries" in times of digital engagement (2023, 69). However, this was not the only factor behind the decision to organize another online version. The 7th edition was viewed as an additional opportunity to experiment with the online format in order to assess if it should be integrated into future editions of NYFAF. As the return to full pre-COVID operations in 2022 was still incomplete, the forum's team once again limited the program to one film, *Myopia* (2020, Morocco), by the Amazigh Moroccan filmmaker, Sanaa Akroud.

Myopia is the story of Fatem, an Amazigh woman, wife, and mother who journeys from her remote village in the High Atlas Mountains of Morocco to the bustling city of Casablanca to have the *fqih*[6]'s broken glasses repaired. Her motive for volunteering for this journey lies in her need to have letters from her husband read by the only person in the village who is literate. Once in the city, she encounters a series of challenging situations and exploitative encounters with human rights representatives, journalists, and the State police that test her resolve, knowledge, and faith. The film delves into various themes related to Amazigh people's connection to their land, spirituality, nature, women's agency and power, education, literacy, and language. Given the richness of its themes, it was decided to stream the film for six days on the LPAC website, while its Live discussion took place on May 3. The panel discussion featured guest speakers from Morocco and different parts of the United States, providing fresh, authentic, and scholarly perspectives. A notable highlight of the panel was the attendance of the film's co-producer and distributor, Mouhamed Merouazi, as well as representatives Sanae Benaadim and Ellen Hernandez from the High Atlas Foundation (a U.S.-Moroccan NGO focusing on participatory sustainable development projects in Morocco). Like the previous online editions, the 7th edition was another opportunity to reconfigure notions of space, temporality, and community in relation to film and cultural events and reach out to a new and diverse audience.

During the three years of the pandemic, NYFAF transitioned from online in 2020, to cancellation or postponement in 2021, to online again in 2022, and then to a blend of an online and in-person format in 2023. The use of a hybrid form of film exhibition for NYFAF's 8th edition seemed inevitable, just as it was for many other film festivals during the post-pandemic period. The first part of the forum in 2023 took place onsite on April 20 featuring the theme of *facing the unexpected* with a program of two feature films in addition to short films. The two features included *Argu* "dream" by Kabyle filmmaker Omar Belkacem (2021, Algeria) and *Sound of Berberia* by Moroccan Riffian filmmaker Tarik El Idrissi (2023, Morocco).

The two films take us on unexpected journeys where the leading characters find themselves facing the unknown. In the first film, the main character, Koukou, is threatened with being sent to an asylum by his fellow villagers for being unapologetically different. In the second film, the characters embark on a trip in search of the diverse music of Tamazgha until they encounter a journalist with unclear intentions. The continuous uncertainty of the characters' destiny in both films largely echoed the long period of uncertainty that characterized decisions and planning around strategies of survival of this cinematic event.

While both films were released during the pandemic, *Sound of Berberia* premiered at the 8th edition of NYFAF rather than at a larger festival, a generous decision on the part of the filmmaker and which was much appreciated by the forum. The onsite version was also enhanced by the presence of Tarik El Idrissi who flew from Morocco to attend the forum in person. During the Q&A session, he sparked educational and enriching conversations with students and other audience members about the diversity of Amazigh musical genres and their impact as a unifying force of Tamazgha. The 8th edition also brought back the music performance session, which NYFAF had previously programmed during the pre-pandemic era. This included a one-hour musical performance by Moroccan Amazigh Abderrahim Boutat, who played the Loutar, a specific musical instrument from the Atlas Region.

The return to in-person events was eagerly anticipated by NYFAF, as they hoped to resume where they left off before the pandemic. Although the morning sessions saw a drop in attendance compared to pre-pandemic levels, the evening showcasing of *Sound of Berberia* helped to restore audience numbers. The return to in-person events provided a moment for reflection on how to creatively improve the forum, and not simply return to its previous iteration.

The second part of the 8th edition was online. The streaming program was available on the LPAC website from April 25 through May 2. It featured a documentary, *Tamorthiw* (Land: Memory for the Future) by the Tunisian Amazigh filmmaker Chahine Berriche (2022, Tunisia), and a feature, *Androman* (Blood and Coal) by the Moroccan filmmaker Alaoui Lamharsi Azlarabe (2012, Morocco). Both films illustrated stories of unseen barriers, risks, and adversity related to the question of gender and the work of memory in Amazigh societies.

The panel discussion, which took place on May 2, covered various topics such as women's cross-dressing in patriarchal societies, women's rights to land through the *Sulaliyyates*[7] movement in Morocco, and the role of oral memory in framing Amazigh identity. The panel featured Drs. Kevin Dwyer and Zakia Salime, who enriched the discussion with their scholarly and insightful expertise on gender equality in the context of Morocco and the current and prospective status of the Amazigh component in Tunisia. During the online discussion, one of the attendees in the chat commented that it was interesting to see Tunisian Amazigh representation on screen as this is relatively unknown.

While physical screenings remain an important part of NYFAF, the forum organizers agree that suspending the online version might not be a wise decision considering the unique cultural exchanges, transnational discussions, and audience reach that the forum cultivated during online screenings. Unwilling to lose such distinct gains, the online version has become an imperative extension of NYFAF rather than a simulation or replacement of the physical screenings. These factors represent a driving force for the continuation of a hybrid form for the 9th edition of 2024, which took place on April 17 and 18 (onsite version) and May 10 to 17 (online version).

6 The Future of NYFAF: By Way of Conclusion

In their analysis of the impact of the pandemic on film festivals, de Valck and Zielinski predict that, in the long term, environmental threats may pose more significant risks than epidemic and pandemic outbreaks. They emphasize the importance of "a growing awareness of the need for structural changes to prevent future ecological disasters" (2023, 308). COVID-19 has presented an unprecedented opportunity to reevaluate the mechanisms, practices, and rationales that have underpinned film festivals from an environmental perspective. Political and economic climates also appear to have had detrimental effects on film festivals. In Tunisia, for instance, Africa's oldest film festival—the Carthage Film Festival—cancelled its 34th edition scheduled to take place from October 28 to November 4 in 2023 in support of the Palestinian people. And in France, the Clermont-Ferrand International Short Film Festival had its regional funding cut in half following a politically motivated decision (Goodfellow 2023). In light of this, it is important to consider the future of NYFAF, particularly as a small-scale, local, and identity-based festival that has not only managed to endure but also flourish during and post-COVID periods despite its limited resources. This chapter's analysis indicates that as NYFAF navigated the challenges posed by the pandemic, attempting virtualization, postponing, cancellation, and hybrid formats, it crafted a distinctive model of resilience and innovation for cultural events in times of adversity. This is particularly evident in its capacity to broaden its audience to viewers around the globe while remaining faithful to its traditional character. NYFAF successfully accomplished this by emulating Q&A sessions, filmmaker and scholar panels, and social gatherings through the virtual version.

It is no longer a valid assumption that only large-scale mainstream festivals can survive critical times. The pandemic has shown us that no cultural event, regardless of its scale, is immune to unexpected disruptions. Similarly, every festival has the potential to survive if it is built on a foundation of commitment, solidarity, and care. It is about those moments of cultural exchange, inclusivity, and that sense of community and connectivity between curators, programmers, filmmakers, and audiences that can help a festival of films focused on Indigenous peoples of North Africa withstand unforeseen challenges. Furthermore, Habiba Boumlik asserts that, "I personally would like to continue this hybrid format because of its convenience and potential to attract a larger audience and perhaps more film submissions" (personal interview with the author, May 31, 2024). As a result, the likelihood of NYFAF embracing both hybrid and physical screenings in future editions as part of today's social and cultural change is higher than ever before. An investigation into the impact of this choice on the goals, mission, and overall landscape of Amazigh cinema would be a compelling area of study. Given that NYFAF stands as a central hub for the Amazigh cinematic expression within the diaspora, exploring its hybridization effects will possibly open new pathways for understanding this emerging genre of North African Indigenous cinema and its cultural significance in a global context.

Competing Interests Research for this chapter draws on research work developed through Social Sciences and Humanities Research Council of Canada Partnership Development Grant #890–2020-0102.

Notes

1. Tamazgha refers to land inhabited by Amazigh people. It encompasses the geographical areas between the Mediterranean Sea and the Niger River, a large swathe of territory spanning Morocco, Tunisia, Algeria, Libya, Mauritania, Mali, Niger, Egypt, the Western Sahara, the Canary Islands, Burkina Faso and Senegal.
2. *Jadaliyya* is an independent ezine produced by the Arab Studies Institute (www.ArabStudiesInstitute.org).
3. https://cdha.cuny.edu/collections/show/372.
4. https://laguardia.catalog.cuny.edu/student-programs-and-ser vices/laguardia performing-arts-center.
5. The Hirak protest movement began in February 2019 when mass demonstrations took place across Algeria opposing then President Abdelaziz Bouteflika's intention to stand for a fifth term. It was characterized by its peaceful and non-violent nature while focusing its demands on political reforms and further freedoms. The movement lasted for about one year until it was halted by the pandemic outbreak in 2020.
6. Fqih is an expert religious figure in Islamic culture(s). In the colloquial spoken varieties of Moroccan Arabic and Tamazight, fqih is used interchangeably with Imam, the leader of religious prayers and sermons.
7. "Sulaliyyates refers to the Sulaliyyates Women's Movement in Morocco, which began in the year 2000. Rural women who lived on collective land demanded equal rights and land shares when their collective land was to be privatized and divided.

References

Boumlik, Habiba, and Lucy R. McNair. 2017. Looking for Amazigh Cinema—Developing the New York Forum of Amazigh Film. *Transnational Moroccan Cinema*. https://moroccancinema.exeter.ac.uk/en/habiba-boumlik-and-lucy-mcnair-summary/. Accessed June 17, 2024.

Brunow, Dagmar. 2020. Come Together? Curating Communal Viewing Experiences for Hybrid and Online Film Festivals. *NECSUS European Journal of Media Studies* 9 (2): 339–347.

Burgess, Diane, and Kirsten Stevens. 2023. Locating Buzz and Liveness: The Role of Geoblocking and Co-Presence in Virtual Film Festivals. In *Rethinking Film Festivals in the Pandemic Era and After*, ed. Marijke de Valck and Antoine Damiens, 59–80. Cham: Springer International Publishing.

Cheyroux, Emilie. 2023. Small Film Festivals Surviving the COVID-19 Pandemic: The 'Virtual Showcase' of Cine Las Americas International Film Festival 2020. *Journal of Festive Studies* 4 (1): 47–65. https://doi.org/10.33823/jfs.2022.4.1.132.

Chun, Wendy Hui Kyong. 2016. *Updating to Remain the Same: Habitual New Media*. Cambridge, MA: The MIT Press.

CUNY Digital History Archive. https://cdha.cuny.edu/collections/show/372. Accessed 10 May 2024.

Damiens, Antoine, and Marijke de Valck. 2023. What Happens When Festivals Can't Happen? In *Rethinking Film Festivals in the Pandemic Era and After*, ed. Marijke de Valck and Antoine Damiens, 1–14. Cham: Springer International Publishing.

Davis, Treviso M. 2021. Film Festivals and the COVID-19 Pandemic: How a Global Health Crisis Changed the United States Film Festival Circuit. *Honors Theses* 1612. https://egrove.olemiss.edu/hon_thesis/1612.

De Valck, Marijke. 2020. Vulnerabilities and Resiliency in the Festival Ecosystem: Notes on Approaching Film Festivals in Pandemic Times. In *Philipp Dominik Keidl, Laliv Melamed, Vinzenz Hediger, and Antonio Somaini*, ed. Pandemic Media, 125–133. Lüneburg: Meson Press.

De Valck, Marijke, and Antoine Damiens. 2023. *Rethinking Film Festivals in the Pandemic Era and After*. Cham: Springer International Publishing.

De Valck, Marijke, and Ger Zielinski. 2023. Greening Film Festivals. In *Rethinking Film Festivals in the Pandemic Era and After*, ed. Marijke de Valck and Antoine Damiens, 307–328. Cham: Springer International Publishing.

Goodfellow, Melanie. 2023. France's Beleaguered Clermont-Ferrand Short Film Fest Could Get "Exceptional" Government Support Following Sudden Regional Funding Cut. *Deadline*. Accessed 19 June 2024. https://deadline.com/2023/05/rima-abdul-malak-clermont-ferrand-short-film-fest-exceptional-support-1235374070/.

Karlekar, Tilottama. 2023. Precarity, Innovation, and Survival in the Indian Film Festival Sector. In *Rethinking Film Festivals in the Pandemic Era and After*, ed. Marijke de Valck and Antoine Damiens, 231–254. Cham: Springer International Publishing.

Kohn, Eric, and Anne Thompson. 2021. Why Major Film Festivals and Studios Aren't Showing Movies Online This Fall. *indieWIRE*. https://www.indiewire.com/video/film-festivals-virtual-fall-2021-screen-talk-345-1234657856/. Accessed 19 May 2024.

Kredell, Brendan. 2023. Scarcity, Ubiquity, and the Film Festival After Covid. In *Rethinking Film Festivals in the Pandemic Era and After*, ed. Marijke de Valck and Antoine Damiens, 41–58. Cham: Springer International Publishing.

LaGuardia Community College. https://laguardia.catalog.cuny.edu/student-programs-and-services/laguardia-performing-arts-center. Accessed 17 May 2024.

Loist, Skadi. 2023. Stopping the Flow: Film Circulation in the Festival Ecosystem at a Moment of Disruption. In *Rethinking Film Festivals in the Pandemic Era and After*, ed. Marijke de Valck and Antoine Damiens, 17–40. Cham: Springer International Publishing.

McNair, Lucy, and Yahya Laayouni. 2021. Amazigh Cinema and New York Forum of Amazigh Film (NYFAF). *Jadaliyya*. https://www.jadaliyya.com/Details/43443.

Negrouche, Samira. 2020. Minus One. Trans. Marilyn Hacker. *Poets.org*. https://poets.org/poem/minus-one.

Olibet, Ylenia, and Alanna Thain. 2023. Vidéo de Femmes Dans le Parc: Feminist Rhythms and Festival Times under Covid. In *Rethinking Film Festivals in the Pandemic Era and After*, ed. Marijke de Valck and Antoine Damiens, 155–175. Cham: Springer International Publishing.

Peirano, María Paz., and Gonzalo Ramírez. 2023. Chilean Film Festivals and Local Audiences: Going Online? In *Rethinking Film Festivals in the Pandemic Era and After*, ed. Marijke de Valck and Antoine Damiens, 129–151. Cham: Springer International Publishing.

Smits, Roderik. 2021. European Film Festivals in Transition? Film Festival Formats in Times of COVID. *Report for Thessaloniki International Film Festival*.

Smits, Roderik. 2023. Disruption in Times of COVID-19? The Hybrid Film Festival Format. *Cultural Trends* 33 (3): 309–323. https://doi.org/10.1080/09548963.2023.2193872.

Vail, James, Theresa Heath, Lesley-Ann Dickson, and Rebecca Finkel. 2023. Film Festivals on the Small Screen: Audiences, Domestic Space, and Everyday Media. In *Rethinking Film Festivals in the Pandemic Era and After*, ed. Marijke de Valck and Antoine Damiens, 81–100. Cham: Springer International Publishing.

Winter, Jeffrey. 2020. A Way of Life in Peril: Film Festival Distribution in the Age of COVID-19. *The* COLLABORATIVE filmmakers first. https://www.thefilmcollaborative.org/blog/2020/05/a-way-of-life-in-perilfilm-festival-distribution-in-the-age-of-covid-19/.

Open Access This chapter is licensed under the terms of the Creative Commons Attribution 4.0 International License (http://creativecommons.org/licenses/by/4.0/), which permits use, sharing, adaptation, distribution and reproduction in any medium or format, as long as you give appropriate credit to the original author(s) and the source, provide a link to the Creative Commons license and indicate if changes were made.

The images or other third party material in this chapter are included in the chapter's Creative Commons license, unless indicated otherwise in a credit line to the material. If material is not included in the chapter's Creative Commons license and your intended use is not permitted by statutory regulation or exceeds the permitted use, you will need to obtain permission directly from the copyright holder.

CHAPTER 6

From Africa to London to the World: Film Africa's Leading Role in the Circulation of African Cinemas

Estrella Sendra and Robin Steedman

Abstract Film Africa is currently the largest festival and meeting point in the UK celebrating the best of African cinema. This chapter probes the festival's goals and how its practices shape the circulation of African cinema in London and beyond. We begin with an exploration of the festival's understanding of "Africa" in dialogue with the festival location. We suggest that the festival adopts an expansive definition, encompassing the continent, diaspora, and those of African heritage. We show that curating Africa in this way serves as a way of acknowledging, embracing, and celebrating the rich and diverse range of cultural heritages that make up the

E. Sendra (✉)
Department of Culture, Media and Creative Industries, King's College London, London, UK
e-mail: Estrella.sendra@kcl.ac.uk

R. Steedman
School of Culture and Creative Arts, University of Glasgow, Glasgow, Scotland, UK
e-mail: robin.steedman@glasgow.ac.uk

© The Author(s) 2025
S. Petty (ed.), *African Film Festivals and Transnational Flows of Living Cultural Heritage*, Framing Film Festivals,
https://doi.org/10.1007/978-3-031-88590-7_6

101

population of London. Through reflecting on field research at the festival as well as with its organizers, we explore how the festival is curated, how the space of London is worked with, and the lessons that can be learned from this festival for other festivals in other contexts.

Keywords Film · Africa · London · Circulation · Cinema · Decolonization

1 Introduction

Film Africa is currently the largest festival and meeting point in the United Kingdom, celebrating the best of African cinema. In this chapter, we explore what the festival aims to do and how its practices shape the circulation of African cinema in London and beyond. We begin with an exploration of the festival's understanding of "Africa" in dialogue with the festival location. We suggest that the festival adopts an expansive definition, which encompasses the continent, diaspora, and those of African heritage. We will argue that curating Africa in this way serves as a way of acknowledging, embracing, and celebrating the rich and diverse range of cultural heritages that make up the population of London. We next reflect on Film Africa's exhibition practices in relation to place. The festival is decentralized and hosted across different venues in various neighborhoods. This practice is a way of connecting to the multicultural and diverse populations in London and very importantly with the various diasporic communities in the city, while also being a way of bringing other audiences to the cinema. The festival is also curated thematically based on where the films will be screened, and this includes multidisciplinary associations such as curating music events and family activities.

We believe that it is possible to see Film Africa as engaged in decolonizing practices because of its curation and exhibition practices, and the ways these are intertwined. Through reflecting on field research at the festival as well as with its organizers (including reflecting on our own roles within the festival over time) we will explore how the festival is curated, how the space of London is worked with, and the lessons that can be learned from this festival for other festivals attempting to engage in decolonizing practices in other contexts.

Scholarship on Film Africa focuses on early editions of the festival (Dovey 2012, 2013, 2015; McNamara 2013; Singer 2013), and thus there is a gap to fill in understanding how the festival operates now, and what is significant about it, over a decade after its founding in 2011. 2011 was also the year in which the co-authors of this chapter were Master's students, taught by Prof Lindiwe Dovey at School of Oriental and African Studies, University of London. As students of Dovey, cofounding director of Film Africa with Namvula Rennie, we were invited to get involved in the festival organization, adopting various roles which later evolved into closer forms of engagement, such as being deputy festival manager and submissions advisor (in the case of Steedman), or advisory board member (in the case of Sendra).

When approaching the festival in 2022 as researchers for the purpose of the Decolonizing Film Festival Research in a Post-Pandemic World project, funded by the New Frontiers in Research Fund (NFRF), Government of Canada, we were aware of how these previous and continuous engagements with the festival shaped our access and approach to it. The analysis that follows is thus informed by these multi-faceted positionalities: as the first generation of class members who voluntarily supported the organization of the first festival; as Film Africa festival-goers and friends with various degrees of practical engagement; as researchers whose interest in African screen worlds was shaped by this practice-based and theoretically grounded learning experience; and, for the purpose of the NFRF research project, as researchers concerned with not just the research outputs, but the process, aiming to find ways of making the research process less extractive and more reciprocal. In this chapter, we reflect on a selection of memories of Film Africa over the years, as well as a series of examples of its exhibition approach in the 2022 edition, which ran from 28 October to 6 November. We further rely on textual analysis of the various catalogues of the festival, with particular attention to curatorial statements. We hope these necessarily brief reflections will invite further scholarship on this festival and decolonizing curatorial practices at film festivals more broadly.

2 Film Africa in Dialogue with the City: Festival Aims

When curating African cinema, both in and beyond the continent, the category of Africa tends to be an "empty signifier" (Laclau 1996). In other words, its meaning is varied, at times vague, and largely shaped by the local context where the festival takes place. In the case of Film Africa, located in London, but also, with a festival name that treats it as a noun rather than as an adjective (the festival could have been named London African Film Festival), Africa is understood expansively, that is, not limited geographically. It refers to the continent, diaspora, people of African heritage, and those who self-identify as African.

When Film Africa was founded in 2011 by activist-scholar Lindiwe Dovey and singer and songwriter Namvula Rennie, with the support of the Royal African Society, the aim of the festival was to showcase the best of African cinema to *London* audiences. The longstanding motto of the festival is "Celebrating the Best of African Cinema". The festival accepts cinema not *about* Africa, but *made by* Africans, including those in the diaspora. The festival's rules for submission state: "Our main objective is to represent a wide range of films and filmmakers stemming from Africa and the African diaspora. We only accept submissions from African and African diaspora filmmakers".[1] Desta Haile, Deputy Director of the Royal African Society at the time of Film Africa 2022, and, as such, festival director, explained:

> The concept of "African" for the festival is both fluid and specific. While the focus is primarily on films from the African continent, it also extends to the diaspora, including black Brits and the Caribbean. While this may not be explicitly outlined, there's a recognition that black American films already have substantial reach and influence. Consequently, the festival showcases African films with an emphasis on diversity, featuring outstanding contributions from black British and Caribbean filmmakers. (pers. comm with Steedman, 2022)

This expansive definition of Africa in Film Africa is thus closely linked to its location: London, which, with 13.5% black British is, according to the 2021 Census, the most ethnically diverse region in England and Wales, and "is historically a city of migrants, defined by the traffic of wealth, goods and people to and through it" (Melville 2020, 15). When co-directors Dovey and Rennie introduced the 2012 festival, they justified its importance with data from the 2012 Office of National Statistics report, suggesting that "London is home to about 400,000 African migrants" (Dovey 2015, 114). That year, audience feedback forms revealed that 29% of the festival audience identified as "black African" and 12% as "black Caribbean" (Dovey 2015, 117). Black African and Caribbean Londoners are not just involved as audience members at Film Africa, but also as filmmakers and jury members of the Baobab Award for short films. Jury members have included well-known black British filmmakers, such as Destiny Ekaragha in 2017, and Shola Amoo, in 2018, to name a few.

Key to the history of migration in London is the British Empire, and the settlement in London by the so-called "Windrush generation", comprised of 60% of people from Jamaica, and this played a key role in "how the city was remade in the late twentieth century" (Melville 2020, 15). Black intellectuals gathered, generating "dreams of pan-African solidarity", fighting for the recognition and visibility of "the African presence in the imperial metropolis" (Matera 2016). London can be considered an "Afro-metropolis", even though the metropolis historically excluded people of African descent and made it difficult for them to find work (Matera 2016). In cosmopolitan yet starkly socially and economically unequal London, artists have been crucial to articulating the various histories of the city (Bradley 2013; Matera 2016; Melville 2020).

The origins of Film Africa and its curation of *Africa* need to be established in dialogue with this context of resistance, recognition, and presence in a postcolonial context of imposed absence by colonial and imperial rulers. As Med Hondo notes, "[t]hroughout the world when people use the term cinema, they all refer more or less consciously to a single cinema, which for more than half a century has been created, produced, industrialized, programmed, and then shown on the world's screens: Euro-American cinema" (Hondo 2023, 165). It is thus no surprise that the first lines of the words of welcome to the first ever edition of Film Africa stated:

> There has never been greater interest in African film. A half-century after Africans started making their own films in the 1960s, supplanting patronizing iconographies, African Cinema is finally being recognized across the globe. (Co-directors Lindiwe Dovey and Namvula Rennie, 2011 Festival catalogue, 2)

When Dovey discusses their efforts to build African and black British audiences for the festival, she is referring to a "principle of responsiveness" (Dovey 2015, 117). This means that, for instance, in 2011, when Mark Duggan, a 29-year-old black British man, was shot dead by the police, leading to protests and rioting in and beyond London, the co-curators decided to screen John Akomfrah's emblematic film *Handsworth Songs* (1986), that focused on anti-racist riots in England almost three decades earlier. This "curatorial strategizing" (Dovey 2015, 118) involved taking a position, carefully thinking of how to facilitate and promote understanding of and engagement with the film, through the involvement of television presenter Henry Bonsu and performance poet Zena Edwards, who facilitated an intense discussion with the audience.

The curatorship and institutional context of the festival has changed over time, maintaining partnerships with venues and expanding towards new festival spaces across the city. Film Africa revised its periodicity from annual to biennial in 2020, alternating with the literature festival Africa Writes, also hosted by the Royal African Society (RAS). The second and third editions (2013 and 2014) were curated by a lead curator, Suzy Gillett, and the 2015 by Isabel Moura Mendes and Jacqui Nsiah, and from 2016 onwards, Film Africa has been an embedded activity of the Royal African Society. Each edition's catalogue features introductory words by the festival producer or Film Africa Team, and since 2022, also by guest curators, invited to join RAS from various points in the African continent to offer a "diverse range of perspectives from Ghana, Kenya and Nigeria", offering stories "from all corners of the African experience" (Aseye Tamakloe, Nyambura M. Waruingi and Wilfre Okiche, 2022 Film Africa festival catalogue, 3).[2]

This shifting institutional context matters. Across our discussions on understandings and practices of decolonization with Desta Haile, a key point arose concerning the organization of the festival and the staffing of the RAS. She suggested, "I perceive decolonization as the active elevation of African voices, perspectives, and diversity. It involves the commitment to hiring Africans whenever possible, which, in my opinion, should always be possible" (pers. comm. with Steedman, 2022). When later questioned about her understandings of practices of decolonization in the organization which hosts Film Africa, Haile added: "In essence, decolonizing is not just about conversations; it extends to institutional changes. At the Royal African Society, it means embedding these values in our policies, ensuring that every step forward isn't followed by steps backward. It requires creating lasting change within the fabric of the organization to make a meaningful impact on civil rights discussions" (pers. comm. with Sendra and Steedman, 2023).

How the festival celebrates cinema—and the events it holds—are sometimes negatively shaped by the festival's very place in London, for example, because of the xenophobic UK visa regime. This was the case, for instance, of rappers Kilifeu and Thiat, who form the well-known group Keur Gui, and who starred in Rama Thiaw's documentary film *The Revolution Won't Be Televised* (2016, Senegal). The artists had been invited to the sixth festival edition, along with the film director, Rama Thiaw, to perform for free at Upstairs at The Ritzy, at the heart of the Jamaican and Black Caribbean capital of the London Borough of Lambeth, Brixton, in South London. The film had been praised for being the first Senegalese production of eighty percent Senegalese cast and crew, and its portrayal of the social movement Y'en A Marre (We are Fed Up), which mobilized the Senegalese population when, contrary to the Senegalese Constitution, then president Abdoulaye Wade announced his intention to run for office again in 2011. However, Keur Gui's visa was rejected, and the performance could not take place. It is common for Africans to be subjected to a strenuous and bureaucratic visa process to enter the UK where it is difficult, in some cases, to even get visa application appointments, much less visas. Even with the Royal African Society's support and invitation, it was not possible for Keur Gui to overcome these obstacles. Film Africa was vocal about the injustice of this visa denial and repeatedly expressed their outrage at the festival. In this case, Film Africa's efforts to connect African artists to London audiences were made impossible because of wider structural inequalities in who can and who cannot gain entrance to the city.

3   Curating and Celebrating the Best of African Cinema

Film Africa takes the position they must facilitate meaningful encounters between films, filmmakers (as well as other artists and speakers), and audiences, and this involves care for their guests. Despite budget constraints, they have sought to maintain high standards of care and hospitality towards guest filmmakers, promoting positive and inclusive experiences for all parties involved. Film Africa's care also extends to their audiences through the thoughtful ways in which they curate a celebration of African cinema.

From the very first edition of the festival, there has been a remarkable emphasis on "celebration". In fact, the first festival was curated and introduced in the catalogue as "a ten-day annual celebration". The curatorial statement of the first edition reflects the meticulous, caring, affective and artisan work involved in the process of hand-picking "the most original work in African filmmaking", organizing a series of discussions and parallel events "to contextualize issues presented in the films" (Dovey and Rennie, Film Africa festival catalogue 2011, 2). We suggest that it is precisely that focus on celebration that involves the festival in decolonization.

If decolonization entails "a radical negation of racism, enslavement, colonialism/coloniality, capitalism, and patriarchy in their past and contemporary forms" (Ndlovu-Gatsheni 2020, 5), Film Africa does so through a promotion of the continent through the celebration of its cinema. It "turns over a new leaf" in the "European game" of representation (Ndlovu-Gatsheni 2020, 5), resonating with the diverse populations of the Afro-metropolis of London. The celebratory dimension of this meeting point for African cinema(s) achieves the degree of unity called for in the process of decolonization. As South African scholar Sabelo J. Ndlovu-Gatsheni puts it: "… unity is the nerve center of decolonization/decoloniality… There is '*amandla*' (power/strength) in unity. There is a revolutionary spirit in unity. There is relationality in unity. There is future in unity (pluriversality)" (Ndlovu-Gatsheni 2020, 15).

As Dovey notes, film festivals with a regional focus on Africa can represent the empty signifier Africa in a more heterogeneous way (Dovey 2015, 113). This resonates with theorizations of decoloniality, as an epistemological process and practice that "undoes, disobeys, and delinks from this [colonial] matrix [of power]; constructing paths and praxis toward an otherwise of thinking, sensing, believing, doing, and living" (Mignolo and Walsh 2018, 4). Film Africa seeks to counteract the misrepresentation and under-representation of Africa, with an explicit acknowledgment that "there is still much work to be done to ensure that African films of all kinds are made visible and available to audiences globally" (Dovey and Rennie, Film Africa festival catalogue 2011).

Film Africa, in the words of Desta Haile while she introduced the screening of *Mon père, le diable / Our Father, the Devil* (Ellie Foumbi, 2021, USA-Cameroon) is "about celebrating Africa, in its beauty and complexity", and this curatorial ethos was certainly on display with this screening. Foumbi's film "interrogates trauma, revenge, survival, loss and other human complexities" (Film Africa festival catalogue 2022, 7). Hosted at Picturehouse Central, the screening was followed by a discussion with the filmmaker in conversation with Carmen Thompson, a film curator previously involved in Africa in Motion, in Scotland, and now working as Programming Director and Audience Manager for the exhibition and distribution company We Are Parable. The discussion with Thompson contributed to contextualizing the film, and to prompting conversations about the representation of trauma on screen. Positionality was crucial to this, and Foumbi shared her lived experience as the daughter of a father who had worked in the United Nations and decided to talk to survivors of the Rwandan genocide, questioning who the child soldiers were. This triggered the question she addressed in her film: How do child soldiers deal with what they had been through? Who do they become when they are adults? It was there that the themes of revenge and guilt, emerged, and led to a screenwriting process that was done, in the filmmaker's words, "from an emotional place", from empathy, and informed by the reading of memories of child soldiers. Even when dealing with complicated subjects such as trauma, the films curated by Film Africa handle these themes "with sensitivity" and are "captured with beauty on screen, reflecting an upswing in technical artistic capacities across the board" (Tamakloe, Waruingi and Okiche, in Film Africa festival catalogue 2022, 3).

Curating discussions with specialist guests, often involving communities of African heritage based in the UK, as well as guest filmmakers from the African continent and diaspora, is typical for Film Africa. This practice of film curation demonstrates and performs the depatriarchization involved in decolonization (Ndlovu-Gatsheni 2020, 7). The festival thus offers an opportunity for African diasporic communities in the UK to celebrate African heritage, placing celebration at the heart of the liberation struggle.

Time, space, political context, and film context all matter in shaping what a showcase of "the best" African film in London would look like. Indeed "representations inevitably play out in particular contexts, and film programming needs to take into account such contexts" (Dovey 2010, 58). Defining "the best" is subjective and there are no undisputed criteria for marking any one film as better than another: rather, what is "best" is *relational*. Film Africa thinks about the best of African cinema in a relational way (films in relation to one another, and films in relation in audiences and spaces). This resonates with Catherine E. Walsh and Walter D. Mignolo's discussion on the role of "relationality" in "embodied conceptions and practices of decoloniality" (2018, 1), and the reminder that we need to stress the role of interdependence in our society, which is pluriversal and should strive for equality (Mignolo and Walsh 2018, 1–2). In the first edition, for example, the catalogue referred to the fact that "more than fifty films... providing a truly continent-wide vision from and of Africa" would be screened at the festival, one "carefully tailored ... along thematic lines" to help move away from the ghettoization of Africa as if it was a homogenous mass.

Similarly, in 2022, the festival's programming goals were to represent the diversity of African culture on screen and to create a program that would resonate with African diaspora communities in London. As stated by Desta Haile, "the goal is to represent a wide range of African countries, ensuring that various cultures and voices are included" (pers. comm. with Steedman, 2022). Aware of the rich cultural diversity in the African continent and diaspora, Haile stressed the relation to place, adding: "In the UK, the communities with the most significant presence, such as Nigerian, Ghanaian, South African, and Kenyan, are particularly emphasized, reflecting the diversity within the African diaspora in the country". Film titles among these included the closing film, *Vuta N'Kuvute (Tug of War)*, a 2021 co-production between Tanzania, South Africa, Germany, and Qatar, directed by Amil Shivji of Tanzania, who was invited to a discussion following the screening with London-based curator Nadia Denton. Film Africa 2022 curator Nyambura M. Waruingi stressed the "conscious effort" made during the selection process "to ensure a balanced representation of the continent" (pers. comm. with Steedman, 2022), claiming: "This involved evaluating how well the chosen films collectively represented different regions. ... The emphasis on diversity, inclusion, and equity went beyond the cinematic appeal of the films. The programming team considered the political and historical contexts of each region, fostering a deeper understanding of the stories being told".

While there has been a strong focus on contemporary productions from the first edition, there has also been an interest in showcasing early film productions. At times this has been to allow these films to be seen after decades of exclusion on global screens. Such was the case of the 35 mm print of *Sambizanga* (1972) at The Ritzy cinema in Brixton in the first Film Africa festival, with the live projection of English subtitles over it, and followed by a discussion with its director, Sarah Maldoror, who made history as the director of one of the first feature length films ever made in Africa by a female director (Dovey 2015, 12). This curatorial decision is reminiscent of the more recent itinerant film program Tigritudes, which reached London screens in 2023, presented as a subjective anthology of African cinema by co-curators Dyana Gaye and Valérie Ousouf, which was also a response to the marginalization of African cinemas from global film circuits (Sendra 2022). In other occasions, the curation of earlier titles has enabled another kind of circulation, re-contextualized and made relevant in the present, either as a heuristic device to reflect on contemporary social or political matters, or to celebrate the work of specific filmmakers. For instance, in 2013, Film Africa curated "3 × 3", a section with a focus on "three directors and their three key films", featuring Mahamat-Saleh Haroun, Mati Diop and Alain Gomis. In the case of Gomis, the festival programmed *L'Afrance / As a Man* (2001), *Andalucia* (2007), and *Tey/ Today* (2012) (*Tey/ Today* was also screened at Film Africa in 2012 with one of its main characters, Djolof Mbengue, as a guest) with a post screening discussion with Gomis. The cross-conversational curatorial approach, putting all three films in conversation with one another, the filmmaker, and audiences, prompted deep engagement with the filmmaker's work and the resoundingly universal theme of migration in his films.

Writing after the second edition of the festival in 2012, Dovey notes: "we hoped to attract London's vast African and black British population to claim Film Africa as their own, and to facilitate other Londoners learning from this community and recognizing its importance to London and the UK's cultural landscape" (Dovey 2013, 122). Ten years later, the desire to reach *both* African audiences in London and those with no connection to the continent remains. Desta Haile explained that festivals like Film Africa are important "not only as showcases of culture for those directly connected but also as opportunities for cultural exchange and understanding" (pers. comm, with Steedman, 2022).

Even though the festival now shares the British Film Institute venue with the BFI London Film Festival, celebrated annually in early-mid October, and just a couple of weeks before Film Africa, the audiences are significantly different. If Film Africa sees a large number of audiences from all ages and, as mentioned above, who self-identify as black Caribbean or black African in over 40%, the BFI London Film Festival has a notoriously less diverse audience that is predominantly white British and of middle-upper age, arguably shaped by the ticket price, which is also significantly higher for the BFI London Film Festival, except for the £5 tickets for younger audiences aged 16–25. We suggest that this difference in audiences is likely because of the care Film Africa pays to creating a festival that black British and African people can "claim as their own" through the films it curates and the diverse spaces it uses. In the next section, we will discuss Film Africa's creative use of space.

4 Engaging Diverse Audiences Through the Decentralization of Film Africa Across London Venues

African film is marginalized in the UK cinema landscape making African film festivals like Film Africa important sites for showcasing it and drawing attention to it. However, alongside the general non-availability of African cinema to UK audiences there is a long and problematic history of African film not being available to African audiences. We agree with Adejunmobi when she states: "One might even say as a provocation, that African cinema refers to those independent feature films that have been more frequently viewed outside Africa than within the continent" (2019, 220). Creating a decolonial future requires rectifying this and making African cinema not just more widely available, but more widely available *to Africans*. As a festival outside Africa, a key contribution of Film Africa in this regard is its longstanding commitment to African diaspora communities and communities of African heritage in London.

Key to Film Africa's practices in this area is the spatial decentralization of the festival across London. Spatial decentralization at festivals is "a caring, audience-centered managerial and curatorial technique in that, instead of expecting audiences to travel to a main venue to be able to participate, the festival travels to audiences" (Sendra 2023, 308). In order to reach diverse populations in London and areas where large African diasporic and black British communities live, such as Hackney and Brixton, the festival decentralizes its venues. In fact, the 2011 festival catalogue emphasized the fact that it was "hosted at the brand-new Hackney Picturehouse", followed by the reference to the four other London venues—"The Ritzy in Brixton, the Rich Mix in Shoreditch, Screen on the Green in Islington, and the Frontline Club in Paddington", a spread which has been expanding over the years (Fig. 1).

Film Africa is an audience-centered festival (Dovey 2015; Sendra 2023), and "to think about audiences also means to think about spaces—the kinds of spaces in which different kinds of people are comfortable or not" (Dovey 2015, 116). Curators/organizers must think carefully about how their desired audience engages with film and the spaces where they engage with it, as well as the barriers that prevent them from coming to new spaces. That audiences love and watch content in *other spaces* does not guarantee that they will come and watch it in a *cinema* (Steedman 2023, 91–92). They need to be convinced to come to a new space, and if the reason is that they *cannot* come to the new space (e.g., it is too

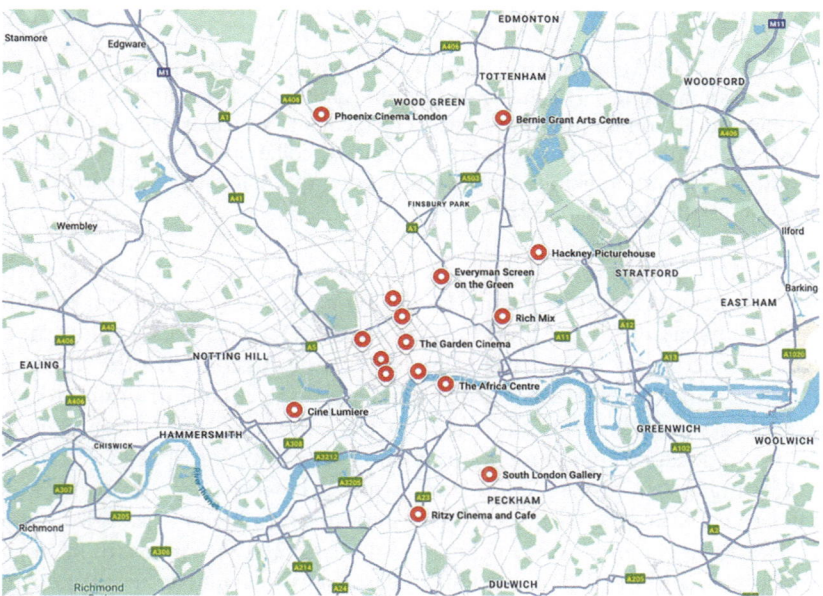

Fig. 1 Map showing the various locations Film Africa has been hosted over the years (*Source* Map elaborated by Estrella Sendra and Robin Steedman for the purpose of this chapter (2024). Courtesy Estrella Sendra and Robin Steedman). [The map can be accessed also via this link: https://maps.app.goo.gl/4UZBk1 PsSW6si37W9] CC BY-SA 4

far, tickets are not affordable), then reaching those audiences requires changing the space.

Film Africa has used non-cinema spaces over the years to reach new audiences and introduce audiences to other ways of viewing film. For example, in the second edition in 2012 the festival had a free exhibition space called "Picha House" in the basement of the Rich Mix, in Shoreditch, East London, that aimed to re-create the experience of an African video hall and which showed political films that "might otherwise not have been part of a film festival-goer's traditional cinema-based experience" if they had needed to be projected on the big screen (McNamara 2013, 128). "Picha House" was thus an experiment in expanding what a festival film could be as well as expanding screening space. Moving beyond cinema space has continued over the years, and is a vital way Film Africa reaches local communities, as Desta Haile said:

> I believe each venue partner plays a crucial role in reaching out to their local communities. For instance, South London Gallery already has an active local community and youth engagement, which is fantastic. The Africa Centre, while not a traditional cinema, collaborated with their chef and restaurant, utilizing their multipurpose space for our event. (pers. comm. with Steedman, 2022)

An illustrative example of this was the "Dine & View" screening (with headphones) of *Amansa Tiafi / Public Toilet Africa* (Kofi Ofosu Yeboah, 2021, Ghana) at The Africa Centre on 31 October and 1 November 2022, preceded by a meal and followed by a discussion with the director. The film director had also brought a bottle of a Ghanaian liquor to the screening space, inviting audiences to taste this typical flavor as part of the multi-sensory engagement sought in this exhibition space.

Getting more diverse audiences requires having more diverse venue types (e.g., non-cinema spaces such as community halls) in a wider range of locations beyond urban centers (Atkinson 2017). An example from Africa in Motion in Edinburgh and Glasgow is instructive here: "During the first six editions of Africa in Motion Film Festival, audiences grew in numbers but did not develop socio-demographically, which can largely be attributed to the festival predominantly being based in arthouse cinemas" (Atkinson 2017, 688). While Africa in Motion initially saw itself as a space for cinema lovers and not diasporic communities (Bisschoff 2013, 147), that changed over time and engagement with diverse communities through participatory programming and venue decentralization became paramount (Atkinson 2017; Van de Peer et al. 2018) (Fig. 2).

In London there is a Senegambian diasporic community very well-known due to their cultural contribution to the city, particularly in music. This is why from the very beginning, musicians such as Gambian kora player Jally Keba Susso or Senegalese kora player Kadialy Kouyate, have been invited to perform at the festival following film screenings. These music performances are often hosted in cultural venues which already engage in audience-centered curatorial techniques, offering events able to resonate and respond to the diversity of the local population. Illustrative examples of these are Upstairs at The Ritzy, in Brixton, where Jally Keba Susso performed in 2012, or the free family friendly multi-disciplinary program held in partnership with Mwalumi Express at Rich Mix, which in 2022 featured Senegalese kora player Kadialy Kouyate and was followed by the screening of the Senegalese film *Les gestes de Saint-Louis / Saint-Louis on the Move* (Kita Bauchet 2021). During the day, there were different "traditional" games with a facilitator explaining how

Fig. 2 Film Africa audiences gathering at the front entrance of Hackney Picturehouse in 2012 (Courtesy Estrella Sendra)

to play them, a marketplace, and food available from Little Baobab, a Senegalese restaurant and catering company founded by the Senegalese musician and chef Khadim Mane, offering a range of Senegalese dishes first in Clapton, then in Peckham, and since September 2024 also at The Africa Centre.

Physical Spaces for talking, mingling, and being together are valuable because they make community, indeed shared physical space is essential to making communities (Kathrin Böhm and Kuba Szreder 2020, 532). A key aspect of Film Africa is that its liveness opens up the possibility for building community. Over a decade after its foundation, the experimentation and proliferation of exhibition spaces has been key to achieving the foundational mission of "redress[ing] this gap between African films and African audiences" (Lindiwe Dovey and Namvula Rennie, 2011 Film Africa festival catalogue, 2). The festival brings African films to African audiences (conceptualized inclusively) in London, but it also helps build community among those audiences—and other attendees of the festival—through the shared act of celebrating films together.

5 Beyond London and Beyond Film Africa: Boosting the Circulation of African Cinema

The decentralization of festival spaces at Film Africa is key to its leading role in boosting the circulation of African cinema(s), both nationally and transnationally. Film Africa has been collaborating very closely with four African film festivals based in the UK, namely, Africa in Motion in Edinburgh and Glasgow, Afrika Eye in Bristol, the Cambridge African Film Festival and Watch-Africa Cymru in Wales. The TANO network (Tano is the Swahili word for five) was founded in February 2013 at FESPACO, where these festivals signed the Ouagadougou declaration to commit to the collaboration and shared mission of bringing African cinema(s) to UK audiences. In 2014, this involved the curation of the film season "South Africa at 20: The Freedom Tour", supported by the British Film Institute and the SA/UK seasons, and running from October 2014 to February 2015 to celebrate and invite reflection on the 20th anniversary of democracy in South Africa.

Coinciding with the festival dates, the five UK-based festivals joined forces to create a UK-wide tour, inviting a series of filmmakers and sharing some film titles, uniquely curated through independent parallel events and speakers organized by each of the festivals in their locations.

In 2016, the TANO network collaborated again with a thematic program of love films, entitled "From Africa, with Love" (2016). This was particularly significant in the mainstreaming of African cinemas, since they were curated as love/romantic films rather than just as African, with screenings extending beyond the festival dates. The catalogue emphasized the universality of the theme, with the following statement: "Is there anything more universal than the power of love?... Across Africa, tales of passion, tenderness, and lust provide intimate perspectives on the diverse and heterogeneous communities of the continent" (Film Africa 2016 festival catalogue, 8). Film titles shared across festivals in this thematic program on love from Africa included *O Grande Kilapy / The Great Kilapy* (Zézé Gamboa, Angola, Portugal, Brazil, 2012), *Love the One You Love* (Jenna Cato Bass, South Africa, 2014) and *Stories of Our Lives* (Jim Chuchu, Kenya/South Africa, 2014), among others.

When the health and sustainability of the festival landscape were threatened by the COVID-19 global pandemic, the festivals did not hesitate to join forces again, curating a retrospective of ten titles, each of them representing the last ten years of the festivals, and entitled WE ARE TANO (we are five), thus also stressing the activist dimension of the festival, and the needed collectiveness in its mission. In an interview on The F-Show, Sheila Ruiz, then director of Film Africa, as the Head of Programmes and Operations at the Royal African Society, said: "Every year we used to share films and filmmakers so that we would create sort of UK-wide tours for certain titles that we all agreed with. We are all independent festivals that have different curatorial approaches, but there are obviously overlaps". This network and collaboration allowed smaller film festivals such as the Cambridge African Film Festival and Watch-Africa in Wales to survive and to offer an exciting film program to their local audiences, with guest filmmakers who would then continue their tours across the UK.

When reflecting about the process of creating the COVID-19 online shared program, WE ARE TANO, Sheila Ruiz claimed:

> We thought a retrospective of the last decade of African cinema would be a great thing to do. We started with this really long list. And one of the very interesting and satisfying things to see was that a lot of the titles that we had screened back in the days that did not have distribution at the time, or maybe they did but didn't really get a long theatrical run, they were now on Netflix, BFI player, or Amazon Prime. That was encouraging to see because these really small five film festivals, we have really contributed

to mainstreaming African cinema in the UK. ... It is not to blow a trumpet but to recognize that our festivals have played a role in that. There's been a shift in what's cool and trendy and there is a huge appetite for African culture and the arts. (Sheila Ruiz on The F-Show, 15 October 2020)

Film Africa has made a vital contribution to "mainstreaming African cinema in the UK" in part through working in concert with other festivals that share its objectives. Through collaborating, its mission to celebrate the best in African cinema has expanded beyond London.

Film Africa's aim is not to remain in London, but to "potentially play the role of better representing African filmmakers, creating more global opportunities, publicity, and greater audiences for filmmakers from Africa" (Dovey 2015, 113). The decentralized London circuit, with multiple screenings of the same film across various locations and mediated discussions with audiences, often with guest filmmakers, further expands across the UK, creating a national flow of African cultural heritage and contemporary artistic work. The TANO collaboration has been crucial to boosting the circulation of these films beyond the UK, thanks to the prestige and added value to the films through the UK-wide film festival circuit. This shows Film Africa's efforts to foster local, national and transnational flows for these diverse representations of African cultural heritage. It approaches curation through a principle of responsiveness both to the social and political context of London and to the local and global (mis)representation of Africa, through a focus on celebration. This entails care, creativity, inclusivity, criticality, empathy, coherence, passion, eagerness as well as guerrilla and grassroots research, which explains the multiple positionalities of curators and team members involved, shifting from practice to research to experience.

6   In Conclusion

Film Africa is a leading festival in the promotion and circulation of African cinema, through an ever-expanding understanding of Africa which encompasses the continent, diaspora, and persons of African heritage. It does so through engaging in a dialogue with the Afro-metropolis of London where it is based, decentralizing its festival spaces and experimenting with exhibition formats, and engaging both African and non-African audiences in the city.

The origins of the festival are anti-racist and activist, which are defining features of decolonization: "decolonization means different things in diverse contexts and there is no one-size-fits-all model", so examining cases of good practice is essential to uncovering what forms of decolonization can look like (Dovey and Sendra 2023, 275, 276). If curators are "cultural gatekeepers", offering contexts to guide audiences through the films, then Film Africa aims to move beyond criticism, by offering alternative representations of the continent and its diaspora that are celebratory of its rich cultural heritage (Ruoff 2012, 2–3). The key decolonizing intervention of Film Africa across its many years has been its steadfast celebration of African cinema and its corresponding acknowledgment, embrace, and celebration of the rich and diverse range of cultural heritages that make up the population of London.

Competing Interests We acknowledge the support of the Government of Canada's New Frontiers in Research Fund (NFRF), [NFRFR-2021-00161] to conduct interviews, a focus group and fieldwork at Film Africa 2022. This project, "Decolonizing Film Festival Research in a Post-Pandemic World", was granted University of Regina Research Ethics Board Certificate of Approval REB# 2022–057 (Nominated Principal Investigator Sheila Petty). Research for this chapter also draws on research work developed through Social Sciences and Humanities Research Council of Canada Partnership Development Grant #890-2020-0102. We are also grateful to Desta Haile and Nyambura M. Waruingi for their time and willingness to talk to us about Film Africa, and to all their colleagues at the festival and the Royal African Society for the access to its various events and spaces. Special thanks also to Prof Lindiwe Dovey, research collaborator in the NFRF project, but also, the force who fostered our interest in this field and festival.

Notes

1. There are other rules for submissions. Notably, films can be any length and genre, but they must be new (see: https://filmfreeway.com/FilmAfrica).
2. In 2024, Keith Shiri, a well-known London based curator, founding member and current chair of the Africa Movie Academy Awards, was appointed Lead Curator of Film Africa.

References

Adejunmobi, Moradewun. 2019. Streaming Quality, Streaming Cinema. In *A Companion to African Cinema*, ed. Kenneth W. Harrow and Carmela Garritano, 219–243. Oxford: Wiley Blackwell.

Atkinson, Justine. 2017. Curating an African Film Festival in Scotland: The Recognition of Difference. *Third Text* 31 (5–6): 681–698.

Bisschoff, Lizelle. 2013. Representing Africa in the UK: Programming the Africa in Motion Film Festival. *Research in African Literatures* 44 (2): 142–162.

Böhm, Kathrin, and Kuba Szreder. 2020. How to Reclaim the Economy Using Artistic Means: The Case of Company Drinks. In *The Handbook of Diverse Economies*, ed. J.K. Gibson-Graham and Kelly Dombroski, 527–534. Cheltenham: Edward Elgar Publishing.

Bradley, Lloyd. 2013. *Sounds Like London: 100 Years of Black Music in the Capital*. London: Serpent's Tail.

Dovey, Lindiwe. 2010. Directors' Cut: In Defence of African Film Festivals Outside Africa. In *Film Festival Yearbook 2: Film Festivals and Imagined Communities*, ed. Dina Iordanova and Ruby Cheung, 45–73. St Andrews: St Andrews Film Studies.

Dovey, Lindiwe. 2012. Report on Film Africa: Celebrating African Cinema, 3–13 November 2011. *Journal of African Cultural Studies* 24 (1): 113–120.

Dovey, Lindiwe. 2013. Film Africa 2012: Reflections. *Journal of African Cultural Studies* 25 (1): 122–127.

Dovey, Lindiwe. 2015. *Curating Africa in the Age of Film Festivals*. New York: Palgrave Macmillan.

Dovey, Lindiwe, and Estrella Sendra. 2023. Toward Decolonized Film Festival Worlds. In *Rethinking Film Festivals in the Pandemic Era and After*, ed. Marijke de Valck and Antoine Damiens, 269–289. Cham: Springer.

Hondo, Med. 2023. What Is Cinema for Us? In *African Cinema: Manifesto and Practice for Cultural Decolonization. Vol. 1: Colonial Antecedents, Constituents, Theory and Articulations*, ed. Michael T. Martin and Gaston Jean-Marie Kaboré, 165–168. Bloomington: Indiana University Press.

Laclau, Erenesto. 1996. *Emancipations(s)*. London: Verso.

Matera, Marc. 2016. *Black London: The Imperial Metropolis and Decolonization in the Twentieth Century*. Berkeley, CA: University of California Press.

McNamara, Joshua. 2013. Thoughts on a Curation of 'the Political' in Film: The 'Filming Tomorrow' Seminar at Film Africa 2012. *Journal of African Cultural Studies* 25 (1): 128–132.

Melville, Caspar. 2020. *It's a London Thing: How Rare Groove, Acid House and Jungle Remapped the City*. Manchester: Manchester University Press.

Mignolo, Walter D., and Catherine E. Walsh. 2018. *On Decoloniality: Concepts, Analytics, Praxis*. Durham and London: Duke University Press.

Ndlovu-Gatsheni, Sabelo J. 2020. *Decolonization, Development and Knowledge in Africa: Turning Over a New Leaf*. London and New York: Routledge.

Ruoff, Jeffrey. 2012. *Coming Soon to a Festival Near You: Programming Film Festivals*. St Andrews: Saint Andrews Film Studies.

Sendra, Estrella. 2022. Dyana Gaye, Réalisatrice—Tigritudes est une anthologie de 126 films d'Afrique de 1956 à 2021. *Le Soleil*, May 30.

Sendra, Estrella. 2023. Traveling to Audiences: The Decentralization of Festival Spaces at the Festival Films Femmes Afrique in Senegal. *Journal of Festive Studies* 5: 304–325.

Singer, Christine. 2013. Film Africa 2012: Education Programme. *Journal of African Cultural Studies* 25 (1): 133–136.

Steedman, Robin. 2023. *Creative Hustling: Women Making and Distributing Films from Nairobi*. Cambridge: MIT Press.

The F-Show. 2020. Film, Media, Broadcasting: How can African Creatives Change the Narrative and Foster and Authentic Voice? Focus on Film Festivals. *The F-Show with Firdoze Bulbulia*, October 15. https://www.facebook.com/watch/live/?ref=watch_permalink&v=771019823742141.

Van de Peer, Stefanie, Lizelle Bisschoff, and Justine Atkinson. 2018. *Africa in Motion: Busting the Canon Since 2006*. MAI: Feminism & Visual Culture.

Interviews

Desta Haile, interviewed by Robin Steedman via ZOOM, 5 December 2022.

Focus Group

Desta Haile (director of Film Africa 2022) and Nyambura M. Waruingi (co-curator Film Africa 2022) with Estrella Sendra and Robin Steedman, via ZOOM, 27 February 2023.

Open Access This chapter is licensed under the terms of the Creative Commons Attribution 4.0 International License (http://creativecommons.org/licenses/by/4.0/), which permits use, sharing, adaptation, distribution and reproduction in any medium or format, as long as you give appropriate credit to the original author(s) and the source, provide a link to the Creative Commons license and indicate if changes were made.

The images or other third party material in this chapter are included in the chapter's Creative Commons license, unless indicated otherwise in a credit line to the material. If material is not included in the chapter's Creative Commons license and your intended use is not permitted by statutory regulation or exceeds the permitted use, you will need to obtain permission directly from the copyright holder.

CHAPTER 7

African Film Festivals: A Transnational Programming Intervention and *Tales of the Accidental City* as a Case Study

Giovana Nabarrete de Souza Cruz and Babatunde Onikoyi

Abstract From 2022 to 2023, three African film festivals in Canada and Brazil engaged in an exploratory transnational programming intervention that examined the impact of a pre-selected film screened at all three festivals. These festivals, held at different times of the year, frame their activities around cultural convergence, connecting filmmakers and audiences, and exploring African living cultural traditions. This chapter examines the outcome of screening Maïmouna Jallow's *Tales of the Accidental City* at the three festivals as part of a programming cycle and intervention. The chapter demonstrates how the film reached a transnational, multicultural level that underscores the divergence in reception due to cultural context, creating a place for discussion between the local

G. N. de Souza Cruz (✉) · B. Onikoyi
Department of Film, University of Regina, Regina, SK, Canada
e-mail: giovana.nabarrete@gmail.com

B. Onikoyi
e-mail: boo919@uregina.ca

© The Author(s) 2025
S. Petty (ed.), *African Film Festivals and Transnational Flows of Living Cultural Heritage*, Framing Film Festivals,
https://doi.org/10.1007/978-3-031-88590-7_7

public at the festival and in the African diaspora. The chapter examines how the tripartite engagement was crucial to the filmmaker's journeys across continents, highlighting beneficial cultural exchanges afforded by such a programming intervention.

Keywords Transnational · Programming · Intervention · Curatorial · Journey · Audience

1 Introduction: Transnational Film Festivals as Sites of Cultural Flows of African Ideas

Film festivals often include films from around the globe in their showings, becoming inherently transnational events where diverse cultures, ideologies, and art meet. As Marijke de Valck has declared, these events are divided into tiers of assumed power: the "A-tier" group, like Cannes, Venice, and the Berlinale, are those that grant the selected filmmaker the highest international prestige (2016, 1). Transnational film festivals can include: (i) co-productions: films produced jointly by companies or individuals from different countries; (ii) global distribution: films distributed and exhibited globally, often with support from international film festivals; (iii) cultural hybridity: films that blend cultural, linguistic, and stylistic elements from multiple nations; and (iv) border-crossing narratives: films that tell stories that transcend national borders, often exploring themes of migration, diaspora, and globalization. By showcasing transnational films, transnational film festivals promote cultural diversity, exchange, and understanding, while also highlighting the increasingly global nature of the film industry.

Any specific film festival, transnational or not, and regardless of size, functions as a site of discourse as it focuses its programming according to its mandate and attempts to attract an audience for the appreciation, analysis, and discussion of the art form. In particular, African-themed film festivals located in the diaspora, propose an extra layer of discourse through a temporary immersion into another cinematic tradition. In a cycle that ran from July 2022 to April 2023, three African-themed film festivals based in the Americas: Vues d'Afrique (Montreal, 2023), the African Movie Festival in Manitoba (AM-FM, Winnipeg 2022), and Mostra de Cinemas Africanos (Brazil, 2022) all programmed Maïmouna

Jallow's debut film, *Tales of the Accidental City* (Kenya, 2021). In fifty-four minutes, this comedy, set in Nairobi, Kenya, probes social justice issues via the stories told by five characters who gather over a Zoom call for a court-ordered anger management class. This chapter explores the festival collaboration and the subsequent results.

Programming intervention or the practice of programming at any African film festival is a crucial curatorial approach that is normally facilitated by festival curators or organizers to bring filmmakers and their works closer to the local audience. For instance, AM-FM targets the local audience and community in Winnipeg, Manitoba, while Vues d'Afrique does the same to its local, Montreal-based audience. Mostra, in contrast, serves more than one local Brazilian audience, as it is almost a "traveling" festival. With segments of its 2022 edition (the one under analysis in this essay) happening in São Paulo, the country's multicultural megalopolis, and others 450 kilometers south in Curitiba, the capital city of the southern state of Paraná, where approximately 74% of the population self-declares as white (IBGE 2022), it has two distinct local audiences. As Lizelle Bisschoff has argued, "programming" as an *engaging* curatorial approach in African film festivals situated in transnational spaces should emphasize "the diversity of filmmaking practices on the continent, and thus incorporates films from a variety of countries, time periods, genres, styles, and themes with film screenings accompanied by a range of events" (2013, 144). A programming intervention within these African film festivals, therefore, brings the local audiences closer to the transnational diversity of the cinematic tradition in question. The members of these communities attend these festivals and, as audiences, have the opportunity to engage directly with the filmmakers and their works through meaningful discussions. Such a curatorial approach is structured to incorporate various activities at a particular film festival while establishing it as an exhibition space and "a market for the media professionals and a medium of interactivity with local communities" (Sawadogo 2022, 37). Directors, founders, and facilitators of transnational African film festivals strive in their collective rationale to develop and create access to African cinema and to provide the right opportunities for African filmmakers to exhibit their films abroad. In transnational cinematic contexts, filmmakers cross borders and establish strategic collaborative relationships with foreign film companies that support their interstitial filmmaking journeys (Naficy 2001; Higbee and Lim 2010; Ellerson 2017). Thus, such a curatorial approach further facilitates opportunities for filmmakers to bond and connect with international investors, who are often capable of creating networks and helping filmmakers promote their works while ensuring other opportunities that will earn them a certain level of global recognition.

Although situated in geographically distinct areas of the Americas, these three festivals share many similarities. As identity-based festivals, they program and curate "with explicit interest in engaging identity questions and representational issues that concern specific communities and groups" (de Valck 2016, 3). Vues d'Afrique and AM-FM, both Canadian festivals, have one significant portion of their audience composed of African immigrants who recognize and connect with the world shown on screen and another of native-born Canadian residents or newcomers of other nationalities who observe African cinema from an outsider perspective. Furthermore, Vues targets a predominantly francophone audience while AM-FM's has been largely anglophone—which provides a different cultural background to each of these Canadian African festivals. Alternatively, Mostra presents African cinema in a country where 55.5% of the population self-declares as black or brown (IBGE 2022), and a great part of the national culture has roots in the traditions of African peoples; so, the films at Mostra present an element of familiarity while the audience maintains its foreign gaze upon them. Beyond (or perhaps in virtue of) the disparities in their audience base, these festivals all developed an analogous mission: to create a dialogue between their audiences and a cinema that showcases unique African perspectives.

Vues d'Afrique, the largest and oldest African film festival in North America, is the most internationally recognized of the three festivals involved in this intervention. For approximately ten days every April, Vues presents its attendees with a mix of screenings, panels, workshops, and awards. Screenings at Vues are managed by a programming committee headed by Kotimi Guira and divided between competitive and non-competitive. In this format, competitive films are submitted to the festival throughout its submission period, while the non-competitive films are invited and selected by specific programmers (and sometimes festival sponsors) with the idea of attracting a larger and/or specific public. AM-FM has the same structure but on a smaller scale; with only three festival days, its screenings, Q&A, workshops, and symposium are compressed into full days of activities over a weekend. It also has in-competition and non-competition films—curated by a jury selected by festival director

Dr. Ben Akoh, with the majority of its programming comprised of in-competition shorts that were submitted and evaluated by a group of programmers. In contrast, Mostra de Cinemas Africanos functions solely on curated, non-competition films. Festival directors and curators Ana Camila Esteves and Beatriz Leal-Riesco are scholars deeply involved in African film research who aim to bridge the lack of African cinema representation in Brazilian film festivals by "bringing to Brazil all relevant titles previously featured at major international film festivals and other noteworthy films identified through the curators' research" (Mostra). Plus, with a duration of about a month and iterations in two Brazilian cities, Mostra runs for the most days per year out of the three in this case study.

The cross-continental screening of *Tales of the Accidental City* was born out of a research project that connected filmmakers, festival curators, and film academics. In July 2022, Maïmouna Jallow's film was independently programmed for Mostra de Cinemas Africanos, in Curitiba. There, Jallow screened her film and led a Q&A session; the audience of fifty reacted strongly to the film, "with both laughter and tears and drawing parallels to the injustices faced by Black and Indigenous communities in Brazil" (Maïmouna Jallow, personal correspondence, 2024). The Brazilian audience related to the African issues shown onscreen, identifying cultural similarities and expressing a curiosity to know more about the African continent and its cinema. Jallow also participated in the 2022 Mostra by facilitating a workshop entitled "I, You, We: telling stories through our bodies, soul, and voice". Running from July 8th to 10th, the workshop created discussions with its attendees on how to assert one's cultural identity through filmmaking with authenticity and boldness. It had a mostly Indigenous and Black Brazilian audience, "and they expressed a deep desire to reconnect with the African continent, through film, storytelling and the arts in general" (ibid.). The event culminated on Sunday with a roundtable discussion with Aïssa Maiga, Jenna Bass, Babalwa Baartman, Ema Edosio, and Maïmouna Jallow on "Independent Production in the African Context" (Mostra 2022).

Dr. Camila Esteves was a member of Dr. Sheila Petty's "Film festivals and transnational flows of living cultural heritage: Africa in the world" research project (funded through Social Sciences and Humanities Research Council of Canada), alongside AM-FM's Dr. Ben Akoh and Vues d'Afrique's head of programming, Kotimi Guira and founder and Président directeur general, Gérard Le Chêne. Through this grant, Akoh was able to travel to Curitiba where he attended Mostra's events and met with Jallow, later inviting the filmmaker to attend AM-FM in September 2022 and screen *Tales of the Accidental City*. At AM-FM, Jallow also had an in-person screening and a lively Q&A of *Tales*. Unlike Mostra, Winnipeg's audience had a large presence of Kenyan newcomers who laughed at different humorous narrative points than other audience members and related their lived experiences with the film's narrative when posing questions to the filmmaker. Overall, the film was warmly received and its Q&A ignited discussions on the vital role social and public structures play in guaranteeing its citizens' well-being, both from Kenyan newcomers who confirmed the onscreen representation as well as Canadians who related it to their diverse Manitoban realities. During that year's AM-FM, Akoh was joined by Esteves, Guira, Petty, Babatunde Onikoyi, and Giovana Nabarrete de Souza Cruz—all participants of the research project.

Nabarrete joined the research project after she coordinated the 2022 Living Skies Student Film Festival (LSSFF), a transnational festival and a site of discourse devoted specifically to student cinema. For that edition, the festival received approximately 1500 short film submissions from around the world, all to be joined in a nine-hour program that spanned over three days at the University of Regina. While curating for LSSFF, Nabarrete watched films from different cinematic traditions that elicited diverse interpretations among the team of programmers. During this process, she observed that subject matter or structures filmmakers used could have their meanings lost in translation, depending on whether the curator recognized the cultural baggage they bring to the screening experience. This issue became evident to her when the other festival coordinators did not understand the underlying political subject matter in the Brazilian short film *A Brisa Que Trouxe* (*The Breeze that Brought You*, dir. Gustavo Koncht, 2021) which to her, as a Brazilian, was most explicit. That realization propelled her to think that a dialogue between films, filmmakers, and audiences that specifically tackled this "cultural gaze" would enhance the festival experience, adding new layers of meaning to the films and rendering the festival as a transnational site of discourse. Thus, driven by her experience at LSSFF, Nabarrete decided to join the Film Festivals research project and attended the 2022 African Movie Festival in Manitoba.

Upon watching *Tales of the Accidental City* at AM-FM, Nabarrete was impressed by the film's transnational social discourse *and* transnational structure; so, she suggested that the film be screened at Vues d'Afrique in

April 2023. This proposition was accepted by Kotimi Guira and so, in a cycle that ran from 2022–2023, Jallow's film was screened at Mostra, AM-FM, and Vues—three festivals that had never worked together before but now shared a transnational flow through a common film. At Montreal, the film was very positively received by the local audience, as pointed out by one audience member who stated it was the first time they had ever laughed that much at a Vues screening (Unpublished notes from Estrella Sendra and Laura Feal, 2023). Beyond appreciating the film's humor, the audience also demonstrated an understanding of Jallow's underlying sociopolitical context. During the post-screening panel, questions and discussions ranged from Jallow's transnational collaboration and process involved in traveling with *Tales of the Accidental City* to curiosity about how mental health issues are currently dealt with in the African continent. Plus, as most of the attendees were women, the biggest discussions revolved around questions on the rise of African women's involvement in film production and how important this participation is, as these filmmakers are able to represent African women's stories and characters onscreen. Finally, crowning her passage at Vues, Jallow and *Tales of the Accidental City* were awarded an honorable mention in the category of Best International Medium or Short Film (Organisation Internationale de la Francophonie 2023).

The reception of Jallow's film was overwhelmingly positive at these three film festivals. Indeed, their audiences attend the festivals and screenings expecting *to interact with African discourse*. While they might not be familiar with it, they presume a structure and narrative that is different from the one found in other non-African-themed film festivals and thus have an open mindset to understand the cultural discourse of the films. However, with *Tales*'s screenings at international film festivals with a broader scope (such as the 2021 edition of the San Francisco International Film Festival), the imposition of a "western gaze" or expectation is possible, leading to confusion or negative responses stemming from the audience's lack of contact with an African framework. A programming intervention that addresses the effects a "cultural gaze" imposes upon viewership experiences would, then, bridge this cultural gap and create an environment for multicultural discourse in these festivals.

After observing the richness of the transnational flow created between Mostra, AM-FM, and Vues through the screening of *Tales of the Accidental City*, Nabarrete then developed a possible cyclical programming intervention between them, where the main goal would be to create a discussion between audiences and filmmakers, fulfilling their role as transnational events that incite cultural exchange.

2 Transnational Programming: Concept and Practice

The intervention was meant to be a "traveling exhibition" of three African feature films, one selected by each of the festivals. This "exhibition" would happen along a programming cycle starting at Vues, as it is usually the first festival in a calendar year, around April. Although the idealized cycle starts with Vues d'Afrique, the programming intervention was developed based on AM-FM's three-day festival structure: two nights for the intervention screenings, and one night for its regular programming. In this model, Vues, Mostra, and AM-FM would each select a feature film and a representative who would travel to the other festivals to moderate a debate between the filmmakers and the public after the films' screenings. This representative could be a festival organizer, local academic, or a filmmaker—as long as they fill the key role of bringing a unique perspective to the discussions on the chosen films. Each festival would thus have a "partner highlight session"—indicating which festival has curated and organized it—as one of their premium screenings, where the selected films would be shown and discussed. In addition, this model allows each festival to screen the selected films an equal number of times.

Tentatively, within these parameters, the programming year between these festivals would have the following schedule: by December, AM-FM, Mostra, and Vues would have selected their films and speakers, and, in April, the program would debut at Vues d'Afrique. Although Vues would not have a "highlight" session at its own festival, the deadline is maintained for them so all the necessary logistics can be arranged between festival organizers. Vues's selected film, then, would "premiere" only in the following stop of the cycle. In April, during two consecutive nights, the specially curated debate and screening from AM-FM and Mostra would take place at Vues. Then, once this festival ends, the next stop would be Mostra, around the middle of the year, in Brazil. There, the same structure would be in place: two consecutive nights with two film screenings (from AM-FM and Vues) followed by discussions. Finally, the cycle would end at AM-FM, with Vues and Mostra presenting their chosen films in Winnipeg. Next, in the following Vues edition, a new cycle of films would be introduced and shared between these festivals.

In their mission statements, the three festivals stress the importance of multicultural exchange in their events, especially in matters of presenting the public with perspectives that may be unfamiliar to them. With this proposed curatorial plan, the audience would be presented with a perspective that is doubly "foreign"[1]: an international production that is deemed important according to the perspectives and values of a non-local peer. Plus, with the open-public discussions mediated by the festival representatives, there would be at least three cultural perspectives arising from the films: the filmmakers', the mediators', and the public's. During the discussion part of the "highlight", the mediators would ask questions to the filmmakers about the cultural baggage the mediators bring to the screenings. This would promote debates that generate community engagement from an audience who does not share the same baggage. Lastly, this intervention would also allow filmmakers to explore how distinct audiences understand and react to their films—the different cultural gazes with which their films are observed. Thus, a dialogue between film, filmmaker, and spectator is created with this programming intervention, adding new transnational layers of meaning to the films and enhancing these film festivals' roles as sites of discourse through multicultural exchange.

Smart7, founded in 2023 by seven European festivals,[2] serves as an example of a successful transnational film festival intervention. The project was funded by the Creative Europe—MEDIA Program, and it consists of "four workshops about programming and audience development, sponsoring and fundraising, promotion and sales, sustainability and green practices as well as an in-competition program of seven feature films, each selected by one of the festivals" (Nowe Horyzonty 2023). With a similar core idea but a different scope to this chapter's proposed intervention, Smart7 serves to demonstrate how collaborative film festival interventions can succeed in creating a transnational flow and dialogue between its participant countries. Furthermore, the project exposes its diverse audiences to their neighbors' cinematic traditions, showcasing their differences while emphasizing that there is an entire European identity that binds them—thus, reinforcing multiculturalism and transforming the festivals into spaces to explore and experience a transnational flow.

3   From Africa to the World: Maïmouna Jallow's *Tales of the Accidental City* as Traveling Film—An African Story Traversing Continents and Film Festivals

See Fig. 1.

In a sense, *Tales of the Accidental City* became the sole "traveling exhibition" between the three festivals under discussion, as a one-film prototype of the aforementioned intervention, bringing Jallow and her film to each festival for a screening, Q&As, and workshops. A Gambian artist with practice mainly in theater, Maïmouna Jallow first attempted to adapt the collection of short stories that inspired *Tales* into a stage play. However, because of the COVID-19 pandemic, she decided to transform this project into her first venture in the filmmaking sphere. The film received national and international attention for its humor, sensitivity, and unusual format—it was edited as if the whole story took place within

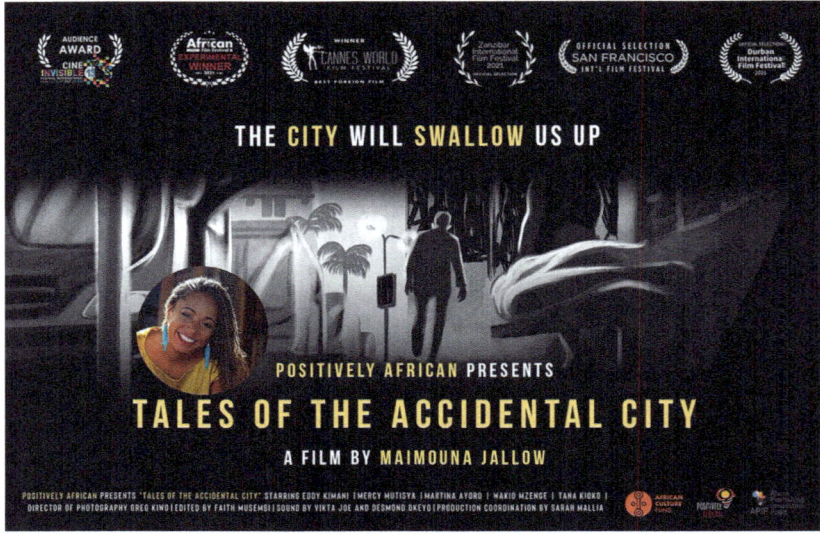

Fig. 1   Poster for *Tales of the Accidental City* with insert photo of Maïmouna Jallow (Courtesy Maïmouna Jallow)

a group Zoom therapy session. At its core, the film represented postcolonial African issues within a Kenyan environment and a universalizing structure. The choice of having the narrative play on a video-call screen made the story contemporary and universally relatable, as the struggles of Zoom meetings were a shared, quasi-global pandemic trauma. Through this intervention, *Tales*'s other international film festival screenings, and its universalizing structure, the film achieved a transnational flow of its postcolonial subtext at various places other than in Africa.

Tales of the Accidental City developed through stages before it was finally produced into a film. The production was conceived when Maïmouna Jallow and a group of artists and writers came together to produce short stories about the city of Nairobi in 2019—an important year for the city because it marked 120 years since its "foundation". Although the filmmaker and her cohort eventually got the stories written, they were unable to publish their stories in an anthology, leading Jallow to consider other ways of realizing the project. Her first idea was to rewrite the story for both radio and then the stage: "But at that time, I was thinking of two things; one was to do a stage adaptation. So, I needed to adapt and stage it as a play; and secondly, to produce it into a dramatized audio version. I received a grant from the African Publishers Innovation Fund to do the audio version" (Onikoyi, Babatunde. 2023. A Conversation with Maïmouna Jallow [Unpublished interview text]). The three-part, 90-minute audio-version production took place during the COVID-19 pandemic; the cast and crew members rehearsed only online and on Zoom. Eventually, the radio drama was ready, and they proceeded to the studio where it was finally professionally produced.

After the successful production of the radio drama, Maïmouna Jallow then decided the time was right for her to do a stage version. She applied for and received a grant from The African Culture Fund to produce a stage play. However, the health measures and restrictions in force due to the pandemic meant the play would have an uncertain premiere and the restrictions turned rehearsals into a challenge. As the stage play became unfeasible, Jallow and her team found a solution: transform the script into a screenplay. As the filmmaker recounts, "After deciding that we would adapt the story for the screen, one of the group members asked an important question: What would an anger management class look like in this period of COVID? It would probably happen on Zoom." (ibid.). And thus, the story turned into a film script centered around four characters: Jacinda, Louis, Diana, and Sarah; all of whom have received court orders to attend a counseling session on anger management with a therapist named Counselor Rose. They meet on Zoom, where each of them shares their experiences and what brought them to counseling.

While the film is very rooted in a Nairobi reality, these characters' experiences could very well have taken place in any African metropolis—and what the filmmaker had in mind during the project's conception was to connect with global audiences. She attempts this connection first aesthetically, by having the narrative play out on a Zoom video call. The Zoom atmosphere is recreated in her film; characters are confined to angles reminiscent of web cameras or a phone's frontal camera; there are "cuts" in internet connection that cause "delays", and an actual Zoom screen is recreated for the audience—as if they were a video-less member of this call. Furthermore, Jallow recreated the call experience by having the characters appear sometimes in screen grid-view and other times in a close-up, reminiscent of the speaker-view in the app, so the character's name and connection status still appears at the bottom of the frame, much like real-life Zoom calls. Due, in part, to this universalizing aesthetic structure, *Tales*' subject matter reaches beyond Nairobi and even Kenya—and is shared as part of Africans' post(neo)colonial experiences.

In addition to the film's aesthetic structure, the narrative thread, built through storytelling as the characters recount their tales of woe, creates a connection with global audiences. Jacinda, the first of the main characters to tell her story, speaks about how she discovered her husband's infidelity, hired a private investigator to track him down in one of his "escapades", and slapped him on the face. Yet, she is the one who faced scrutiny from her peers and was ordered an anger management session by the court, while her husband continues unpunished. Diana's story follows Jacinda's as she narrates the kidnapping of her daughter, Nina. The kidnapper posed as a cloth seller in a nearby neighborhood and lured Nina into her establishment. Diana tries but receives no help from the local authorities; thus, she takes matters into her own hands, tracks down the kidnapper, and beats them blind with a stone. The third person, Louis, was sent for counseling after he had hit a dog with his car when he was seen speeding off from a press interview, where a corruption scandal was being revealed. Sarah, the last to tell her story, confesses she was sexually assaulted and impregnated by a policeman, who neglected the child and, since Sarah had no means of raising them on her own, had to give the infant up for adoption. Hence, as each character recounts their personal situation, the audience's empathy towards them grows.

With this narrative structure, spectators realize that, although the characters seem in control of their actions, their outbursts of anger were provoked by a series of state structural failures. The police who would do nothing for Diana's case, Louis's corruption case and further expulsion from city council, Jacinda's husband suffering no consequence (beyond her slap) for his infidelity, and Sarah having to give up her child exemplify that the root of their problems could be solved if a present and caring state functioned equally for all its citizens. At each narrative turning point, it becomes clearer that the societal structures led the characters to these points in their lives—an "anger management" therapy session, following their rebellion, in their ways, against the structure that failed and oppressed them.

In this film, Maïmouna Jallow paints the city as inextricably linked to the postcolonial problems of helpless citizens, who day after day suffer from hardships that have been created, nurtured, and sustained through nefarious acts of postcolonial corruption. Nairobi is depicted as a corrupt and dangerous space that ignores those who cry out for justice. Nonetheless, the filmmaker's narrative and aesthetic structural choices aided in making the subject matter of corruption and inequality transnational. The local audiences from Mostra, AM-FM, and Vues recognized the underlying theme of social breakdown and urban corruption in the film and could relate it to their lived experiences. Thus, the different cultural contexts within which this film was screened effected African transnational discourse, already a defining feature of African cinematic traditions.

4 Conclusion

Despite its Nairobi, Kenya setting and its distinctly African thematic concerns, Maïmouna Jallow's *Tales of the Accidental City*'s trajectory across transnational festival circuits in North and South America underscores its universal appeal, resonating with audiences in Canada and Brazil. The film's exploration of pressing issues—kidnapping, gender violence, policing, political corruption, and religiosity—transcends geographical boundaries, facilitating a profound connection with diverse viewers, creating a multiplicity of transnationalisms, thereby redefining the parameters of cinematic engagement.

The intervention between Vues, Mostra, and AM-FM succeeded in creating a transnational flow and joining festivals and filmmakers around one film. It is worth noting that the structure of the film added a universalizing factor, as the Zoom meeting (and the film itself, which ironically would not have happened if it were not for the pandemic) was a format that local audiences could relate to—which aided in the interpretation of the postcolonial discourse presented within the film. In addition, anger and frustration are universal feelings, as well as dispossession and the feeling that the "little guy" gets a raw deal in the capitalist systems that rule the world. This is why the audiences in Brazil, Canada, and further afield could identify with the story. Ultimately, the cultural exchange in these diverse sites of discourse expanded the film's meaning and developed new layers of interpretation. Thus, Jallow's case served as a representation of the possibility transnational programming interventions can bring to identity-based film festivals and filmmakers who take part in them.

Maïmouna Jallow's film at Vues, AM-FM, and Mostra also gives prominence to the cultural wealth of the continent in diaspora to further expand the knowledge about the continent for the second generation of Africans in Brazil and Canada and in other diasporic communities. Jallow accomplishes this by using the three festivals as a set of conduits to open up dialogue between Africans, Afro-Canadians, and Afro-Brazilians. The programming intervention has become a constituent framework that helps the audience to come to terms with the importance of Maïmouna Jallow's work as significant to African cinema and transnational flows of discourse. Such discourse underscores the need for more engaged scholarship around the importance of "programming interventions" that honor African cinema and social change—which is relevant to African lives and agendas—both in Africa and in the diaspora. The festival space is the site of interaction where all this is happening and *should* continue to happen. As Cindy Hing-Yuk Wong argues, film festivals "promote cinemas that articulate different experiences and expressions, and in doing so, they constitute alternative public spheres/counterpublics where ideas, often-times repressed or ignored in larger contexts, are exchanged and explored" (Wong 2011, 160). Transnational programming interventions, such as the one under discussion in this chapter, enhance this festival characteristic by proposing this exploration and exchange.

The prototype programming intervention between Mostra de Cinemas Africanos, African Movie Festival in Manitoba, and Vues d'Afrique successfully added complexity to the festivals' transnational flows. Such an idea arose from the desire to recognize the cultural gaze imposed by audiences and filmmakers upon the films they watch at transnational film festivals. Yet, instead of asking these groups to "ignore" this gaze, the intervention proposed to create a discussion and cultural exchange between the parts. *Tales of the Accidental City*, a living cultural product born out of the Nairobi environment, provided a blueprint for a possible bigger, more comprehensive intervention between these festivals. The combination of universalizing structures in Maïmouna Jallow's film with an unprecedented cross-continental African film festival partnership elicited discussions within the local audiences and added new layers of meaning to the film, the filmmaker, and her work. Thus, this tripartite engagement established these festivals as sites that not only showcase transnational discourses but also engage with and encourage them.

Competing Interests Research for this chapter draws on research work developed through Social Sciences and Humanities Research Council of Canada Partnership Development Grant #890-2020-0102.

Notes

1. "Foreign" is applied in this context because it refers to the cultural environment of the festival venues. Although there might be audience members for whom the films' worlds are not foreign, the perspectives presented at the discussions by the other festival representatives will be.
2. Members: New Horizons International Film Festival (Poland) as coordinator, FilMadrid (Spain), Thessaloniki International Film Festival (Greece), IndieLisboa (Portugal), Vilnius International Film Festival KINO PAVASARIS (Lithuania), Reykjavík International Film Festival (Iceland), Transilvania International Film Festival (Romania) (European Commission 2023).

References

Bisschoff, Lizelle. 2013. Representing Africa in the UK: Programing the Africa in Motion Film Festival. *Research in African Literatures* 44 (2): 142–162.

De Valck, Marijke. 2016. Introduction: What Is a Film Festival? How to Study Festivals and Why You Should. In *Film Festivals: History, Theory, Method, Practice*, ed. Marijke de Valck et al., 1–12. Oxon: Routledge.

Ellerson, Beti. 2017. Traveling Gazes: Glocal Imaginaries in Transcontinental, Transnational, Exilic, Migration, and Diasporic Cinematic Experiences of African Women. *Black Camera* 8 (2): 272–289.

European Commission. 2023. Commission Supports European Audiovisual Festivals. https://digital-strategy.ec.europa.eu/en/news/commission-supports-european-audiovisual-festivals. Accessed 3 February 2025.

Higbee, Will, and Lim Song. 2010. Concepts of Transnational Cinema: Towards a Critical Transnationalism in Film Studies. *Transnational Cinemas* 1 (1): 7–21.

IBGE. 2022. Tabela 9605: População Residente, Por Cor Ou Raça, Nos Censos Demográficos. https://sidra.ibge.gov.br/Tabela/9605. Accessed 1 June 2024.

Mostra de Cinemas Africanos. About. https://mostradecinemasafricanos.com/en/sobre/. Accessed 1 June 2024.

Mostra de Cinemas Africanos. 2022. 2022 | Curitiba. https://mostradecinemasafricanos.com/en/acervo/curitiba-2022/. Accessed 1 June 2024.

Naficy, Hamid. 2001. *An Accented Cinema: Exilic and Diasporic Filmmaking*. Princeton: Princeton University Press.

Nowe Horyzonty. 2023. SMART7—A network of European Fresh Visions and Team Empowerment (SMART7). https://ec.europa.eu/info/funding-tenders/opportunities/portal/screen/how-to-participate/org-details/999999999/project/101093512/program/43251814/details. Accessed 3 February 2025.

Organisation Internationale de la Francophonie. Palmarès Vues d'Afrique Montréal 2023. https://www.imagesfrancophones.org/actualites/palmares-vues-d-afrique-montreal-2023. Accessed 30 June 2024.

Sawadogo, Boukary. 2022. FESPACO and Critical Discourse on African Cinema. *Journal of African Cinemas* 14 (1): 35–47.

Wong, Cindy Hing-Yuk. 2011. *Film Festivals: Culture, People, and Power on the Global Screen*. New Brunswick, New Jersey, and London: Rutgers University Press.

Open Access This chapter is licensed under the terms of the Creative Commons Attribution 4.0 International License (http://creativecommons.org/licenses/by/4.0/), which permits use, sharing, adaptation, distribution and reproduction in any medium or format, as long as you give appropriate credit to the original author(s) and the source, provide a link to the Creative Commons license and indicate if changes were made.

The images or other third party material in this chapter are included in the chapter's Creative Commons license, unless indicated otherwise in a credit line to the material. If material is not included in the chapter's Creative Commons license and your intended use is not permitted by statutory regulation or exceeds the permitted use, you will need to obtain permission directly from the copyright holder.

CHAPTER 8

"Act in Your Location, Think with the World": Constructing Audience "Afterlives" at Three North American-Based African Film Festivals

Sheila Petty and Estrella Sendra

Abstract This chapter focuses on three African film festivals/programs located in Canada and Mexico. Beginning with an examination of the longest-running African film festival in Canada—Vues d'Afrique—in

---

We borrow this term from Édouard Glissant, "Agis dans ton lieu, pense avec le monde", *Philosophie de la Relation*. Paris: Gallimard 2009, 87.

S. Petty (✉)
Department of Film, University of Regina, Regina, SK, Canada
e-mail: Sheila.Petty@uregina.ca

E. Sendra
Department of Culture, Media and Creative Industries, King's College London, London, UK
e-mail: Estrella.sendra@kcl.ac.uk

© The Author(s) 2025
S. Petty (ed.), *African Film Festivals and Transnational Flows of Living Cultural Heritage*, Framing Film Festivals,
https://doi.org/10.1007/978-3-031-88590-7_8

Montreal, the chapter also explores a relatively new festival in Winnipeg—African Movie Festival in Manitoba, and finally a very recent initiative in Mexico to bring African films to Afro-Mexican communities. The chapter explores selected "afterlife" events of the festivals that are organized to build year-round sustained audience bases and community impact through Bill Reid's notion of artworks (festivals) as "lives" and the community dialogues and events surrounding the works as "afterlives". We envision festival afterlives, not in the sense of negative residue of colonialism or slavery, nor as legacy activity, but more as a relationship between filmmakers, audiences, and films, that is paramount to building communities and social networks off-screen in local communities and throughout the diaspora.

Keywords Afterlife · Global · Local · Place · Community · Festival

1 Introduction

Scholarship on film audiences has, until more recently, mostly focused on the role of the spectator vis-à-vis the screened text and in concert with the role of the author/filmmaker and their artistic intent. With the rise of academic research and non-academic work on film festivals, the focus on viewership has become imperative as audiences are the cornerstones of festivals. Attracting "the largest possible audience" for festival events is one of a programmer's most difficult challenges, according to Peter Bosma, who also maintains that programmers act as "custodians of cinema culture" (2015, 1). Since a festival can hardly exist without an audience, Bosma insists that drawing large festival viewership involves consideration of the context of "local film culture" when designing a program (2). Curator and researcher Farah Clémentine Dramani-Issifou takes Bosma's point further and suggests that film curating "is located between caring for the film and being concerned about the impact of the films" (2023, 257). To her, curators need to commit to filmmakers, producers and audiences alike, "interven[ing] in local issues and communities to invent a new 'mondialité' (Glissant 1997)" (Dramani-Issifou 2023, 264–265).

In her research on African film festivals, Lindiwe Dovey writes that she is concerned with how audiences are "both abstract (in terms of how they are imagined by festivals and curators) and grounded (in terms of fieldwork I have conducted at different film festivals in distinct locations with specific spectators)" (2015, 11). Organizing venues and spaces for meaningful engagement of screen media by audiences is also the work of festival programming and, as Roya Rastegar puts it, "the exhibition structure of a festival impacts which audiences attend, how they watch the films, and what kinds of engagements they make with each other before and after screenings" (2016, 189). Creating one's own screening space and relationship to and with it, will be different for different audiences in different contexts. Rastegar points out that June Givanni maintains this is paramount for audiences of color who connect with productions by, for, and about them and thus participate in "creating the contexts for 'new social viewing experiences'" (2016, 189). Pamela Wilson writes that many Indigenous cultures value "collective authorship and input into a cultural production" thus "blurring the line between producer and audience" and foregrounding the importance of community (2016, 91).

Dovey extends this thinking by offering two principles of screen curation. First, she urges festivals to meet their audiences halfway through co-curation and by "incorporating audiences in film curatorial practices" thus creating what she calls, "(dis)sensus communis" (2015, 153). She thus argues for turning the process of meaning making on its head, promoting a pathway through which meaning is created through disruption of the status quo, rather than meaning being forged solely through an organized system. Second, she describes "the need to challenge local audiences with new ways of looking at and thinking about the world" (153). These principles align with Glissant's theorization on "tout-mondisme" and contribute to the development of a methodological framework for thinking about remapping the world through transnational and globalized forms of cultural contact (2009, 87).

Audiences have a stake in this constantly unfolding process, and, as Pamela Wilson writes in the case of Indigenous festivals, concepts such as "audience" and "community" are already organically embedded in the very production of the event's cultural sovereignty (Wilson 2016, 91). The issue for many festival organizers is how to sustain audience interest in the festival beyond the time and space of the actual event? This requires process and relational thinking and organizing rather than a static state way of being, that carries on after the life-span of an event. Jacques Derrida views this process, not as a static state or theory, but as a form of "survivance" or "afterlife" and "the surviving of an excess of life which resists annihilation" (1996, 60). From this reasoning, festival "afterlives" could include year-round activities or auxiliary activities that accompany a festival: art exhibitions, conferences, and training programs. Festival afterlives, should therefore be envisioned, not in the sense of negative residue of colonialism, nor as legacy activity, but more as a relationship between filmmakers and audiences and a relationship between filmmakers themselves (Dovey 2015, 100).

The network of filmmaker-film-spectator is paramount to building communities and social networks off-screen in local communities and throughout the diaspora. The late Haida artist and master carver Bill Reid, when writing about Indigenous Northwest Coast art, outlined how an artwork/film's "real life" is the process and movement through which it becomes a work, but its "afterlife" is constructed during readings of and engagement with the work through shared participation in local and diasporic cultural manifestations (Reid 2000, 71). In this chapter, we take up Bill Reid's articulation of "the relationship between contemporary viewers, like himself, and what he calls the 'high art of the Indian past'" (Reid quoted in Allen 2012, 2). Reid argues that contemporary engagement, "enriched by a knowledge of the world's art" allows for the uncovering of even greater meaning than was originally intended by the artist or creator (2). The chapter focuses on three African film festivals/programs located in Canada and Mexico. Beginning with an examination of the longest-running African film festival in Canada—Vues d'Afrique—in Montreal, the chapter then explores a relatively new festival in Winnipeg—African Movie Festival in Manitoba, and finally a very recent initiative in Mexico to bring African films to Afro-Mexican communities. Each festival was created with local audiences at the forefront of its mission, thus navigating the landscape of local populations and languages. The chapter explores selected "afterlife" events of the festivals that are co-curated or community-organized to build year-round sustained audience bases and community impact, grounded in Bill Reid's notion of artworks (festivals) as "lives" and the community dialogues and events surrounding the works as "afterlives".

2 Rallye-Expos and Vues d'Afrique

Festival International de Cinéma Vues d'Afrique is the longest running African film festival in North America. It has been held annually in April/May in Montreal since 1985 with a mission to bring African and Creole artistic and cultural production to Quebec audiences and to forge transnational screen media partnerships, relationships, and spaces of exchange of ideas and experiences between filmmakers from the African continent and local Québécois filmmakers who are interested in this region of the world.

The first edition was a veritable who's who of African cinema and was held at two venues that became familiar locations for the festival over the years: Cinémathèque québécoise and the ONF (Office national du film du Canada) in Complexe Guy Favreau. The program included a panorama of films from the 1960s-1980s, directed by first and second generation African filmmakers including: Ousmane Sembène (Senegal); Gaston Kaboré and Idrissa Ouédraogo (Burkina Faso); Gnoan M'Bala (Ivory Coast); Souleymane Cissé and Cheick Omar Cissoko (Mali); Férid Boughedir, Taïeb Louhichi and Nacer Khemir (Tunisia); Nabyl Lahlou (Morocco); and Brahim Tsaki (Algeria). These filmmakers were all present along with several personalities such as: Alimata Salembéré (representing FESPACO, Burkina Faso),Tahar Chériaa (founder of Journées Cinématographiques de Carthage, Tunisia) and Jean-Pierre Garcia (Director of Journées Cinématographiques d'Amiens, France), who were present at the first edition to establish transnational partnerships with Vues d'Afrique and dialogues between African and Québécois filmmakers (Gérard Le Chêne 2024, 10–11).

The festival has grown exponentially over the years and now hosts many artistic and cultural events year round such as public moonlight screenings in Montreal's famed Parc Lafontaine; film production and screenwriting training workshops for elementary and secondary school students in Montreal and on the African continent; three location screenings from Africa to Haiti to Montreal. These are natural audience builders for the main event, the festival itself, which had also served as a documentation center for scholars and the general public, until the tragic fire of May 2023 when the Monastère du Bon-Pasteur, a monastery in central Montreal that dates back nearly two centuries and was classified as an historical monument by the Quebec government, was severely damaged by the fire. This was the location of the offices of Vues d'Afrique where the festival archives were stored.

Vues d'Afrique has been, from the very beginning, a staunch promoter of all visual arts. From the very first edition a competition was launched for the poster of the Vues d'Afrique Film Festival. This competition was reserved for artists of Afro-descendants and another rule of the competition was that applicants were asked to present their artistic portfolios, rather than a poster design. The chosen artist would then work in collaboration with a graphic designer to create the festival edition's poster, the design of which would also grace the cover of the year's catalogue, program and postcards, all of which have become collectors' items. The chosen artist is profiled during press conferences and other events as part of the year's edition. Many of the artists who created designs for the festival posters still reside in Montreal, but Akatia Banvo, the artist who created the design for the first edition's poster, returned to Ivory Coast and runs an art gallery in the tourist village of Grand Bassam.

Vues d'Afrique's desire to provide more space to the visual arts led to the creation, in 1994, of the "Rallye-Expos". Curated by Algerian-Canadian curator, Bousmaha Seddiki, this major event is held annually from the beginning of Black History Month on February 1 to June 30 and offers audiences the opportunity to discover works of photography, sculpture, painting, and mixed media by artists of African and Creole descent, especially from Quebec and Canada, and places and spaces around Montreal from the large musuems to art galleries and trendy cafes. In 2024, fifteen exhibitions were organized during the five months of the Rallye. Members of the public can pick up a "passport" at the Vues d'Afrique offices or any of the exhibition venues, have the passport stamped at each exhibit visited and return the passport to Vues d'Afrique for festival tickets and passes. In 2024, five stamps garnered two festival tickets; eights stamps garnered a festival pass for four screenings; and ten stamps garnered a "cine" pass for ten screenings. On the occasion of the festival's fortieth anniversary, Seddiki and Vues d'Afrique organized an exhibition of the festival's forty posters from June 3–30, 2024 at the Maison du Conseil des Arts de Montréal (see Fig. 1). This formula is a real success, a win-win for all because both the festival and the exhibition venues benefit from "grounded audiences" who will likely attend both exhibits and films and, in turn, contribute to ongoing, sustained dialogue about what it means to be African in contemporary society (Dovey 2015).

3   African Movie Festival in Manitoba

Since its first edition held in May 2018 (subsequently during the third weekend in September), the African Movie Festival in Manitoba has presented African feature and short film screenings, director interviews, themed symposia, and curated entertainment for screen media audiences in Winnipeg, Manitoba. Founded in 2017, by Dr Ben Akoh, the festival

Fig. 1 Poster for "Vues d'Afrique—40 Ans d'Affiches" exhibition at Maison du Conseil des Arts de Montréal during the Rallye-Expos 2024 (Courtesy Vues d'Afrique)

"showcases the best of African Cinema and creates a platform for Afro-Canadian dialogue" to engage the large, diverse and growing African population in the city. Furthermore, the curatorial team and festival organizers are all African or Afro-descendant (personal comm with Petty, 17 January, 2023).

Although the festival screens mainly English-language or English-subtitled films, Akoh's goal is to diversify and each edition has screened several French language films. This is a welcome feature for the large African francophone population of Winnipeg, a city that is also home to the francophone university, Université St. Boniface, which attracts many African students and faculty. The evolving composition of the festival's demographic landscape to include more African-Canadians, and the goal to reach the city's many Indigenous citizens has meant reevaluating the festival's curatorial thrust to encourage transnational dialogue between filmmakers and audiences within a decolonizing goal of offering pan-prairie (Canadian and American) audiences stories through "the lens of an African perspective" and to put "power in the hands of people that otherwise would not have the power to determine what that should look like and how that space can be and grow as a part of the process" (personal comm with Petty, 17 January, 2023). Thus, the festival itself is a structure that challenges colonial spaces since all decision-making is in the hands of Africans and Afro-descendants. Furthermore, the festival is also a place/space of both "abstract" and "grounded" audiences in Dovey's terms, because cultural exchange extends beyond the confines of the city of Winnipeg. For example, classes of film students at the University of Regina attend the festival virtually and write film reviews as class assignments. This is part of the pan-prairie focus that has been a goal of festival director Ben Akoh since its inception.

In concert with his decolonizing goal of offering stories by, for, and about Africans, Akoh has also developed two interesting and innovative examples of "afterlives" that function to build audiences though a pedagogical lens of teaching and "giving back" to the people with whom one works and lives, a principle of reciprocity embedded in Indigenous epistemology. The first "afterlife" example is the symposium organized and held during each edition of the festival. The aim of the symposium at each edition is to highlight the social, political and cultural environments portrayed in African and African diasporic films and to link these themes to issues in Manitoba and Canada. Films are then curated to speak to the festival theme(s). During the first edition, on May 5, 2018, the symposium addressed the topic of "African Cinema and Multiculturalism in Manitoba," and topics have evolved over the years but are always linked to the idea of "place" in order to draw in both academic and community audiences. A major strength of the festival lies in Akoh's ability to bring together various proponents of local municipal and provincial governments and communities with academic scholars. In 2022, keynote speaker and acclaimed Nigerian filmmaker, Tunde Kelani, addressed the topic of "African Films and the City: Space-making, Place-making, Film-making" via Zoom, creating an interesting "abstract" transnational space with audiences between Nigeria and Canada. His talk reinforced how African cities often serve as much more than a background in the films' stories but also often represent both a remnant of colonization (as colonial metropoles) and an opportunity for cultural place-making, belonging and hope, but also as places of marginalization. The focus on film and the city invited critical dialogue on the important place that cities occupy in the world of African films, and on the kinds of social, economic, political and cultural conditions of African lives and experiences, and the experiences of Africans in diasporic cities, especially in those of Manitoba and Canada more broadly. The symposium theme for 2024 was "African Popular Arts and the Discourse of Migration", with a keynote by Dr. Paul Ugor, University of Waterloo, and held in concert with the national conference, "Contemporary African Migration to Canada: New Directions, Approaches, Theories". The latter, organized by festival advisory committee member, Dr. Chigbo Anyaduba, at the University of Winnipeg, was a first-of-its-kind national conference that brought together academics, students, community organizations, and policy makers to discuss issues pertaining to contemporary African migration to Canada. The 2024 conference was particularly timely as it coincided with the end of the United Nations International Decade for People of African Descent (2015–2024), providing an opportunity to consolidate dialogue in the field of African migration and diasporic studies, with a specific focus on Canada (Fig. 2).

The second "afterlife" example is the AM-FM Filmmakers Masterclass, an intense workshop that fosters future talent. The workshop has been held four times: twice during COVID-19 in 2021; once in 2022/3, and most recently in 2024. A call goes out on social media and via direct email to African community associations. The criteria for acceptance is self identification as black, preferably African, living in Manitoba and available to fully participate in person. Funded provincially by the Manitoba Arts Council, an arms length government funding agency for the arts, thirteen emerging black filmmakers (must be age 15 or older) were chosen in 2024 for the workshop which lasted eight weeks spread over two–three months. Students were taught the crafts of screenwriting, directing, and cinematography, and post production film business management. The film shoot took one day and post production took a couple of weeks, in addition to the eight week workshop. Instructors included a seasoned director, a screenwriter, and a cinematographer. The final product was the collaborative eight-minute film, *Misinterpretation* that was screened to much acclaim during the festival, with advice and support offered by filmmakers Meg Rickards (South Africa) and Sunita Miya Muganza (Canada) who were in attendance at the festival for their own films. By the end of the masterclass, the students had produced thirteen different

Fig. 2 2024 Poster for African Movie Festival in Manitoba (Courtesy African Movie Festival in Manitoba)

short screenplays. Funding was obtained to produce one more screenplay after *Misinterpretation* and production on this project is currently underway. The plan, according to Akoh, is to have all thirteen shorts produced, dependent on available funding (personal comm with Petty, September 29, 2024).

In four short years, the masterclass has successfully trained young filmmakers to develop their creative and critical skills, to realize their unique paths and to take their places in the artistic world and digital media industries. A couple of young filmmakers from previous classes have gone on to study filmmaking at university and college levels. Together, the symposia and masterclass programs build audiences for the festival itself and continue to "give back" to the communities that have supported them.

4 The Black Pacific: Exploring the Afterlives of the Festival Artístico Audiovisual Afrodescendencias in Costa Chica (Mexico)

The Festival Artístico Audiovisual Afrodescendencias was founded in 2021 by a group of researchers, artists, activists and communities in order to celebrate Afro-Mexican identity through a multidisciplinary and itinerant showcase of Afro-Mexican arts.[1] In June 2024, it hosted its fourth edition across three different areas in Costa Chica, Cuajiniculapa and El Quizá (Guerrero) and Lo de Soto (Oaxaca).[2] Due to their geographic location, in the border between Guerrero and Oaxaca, and near the coast, these regions are particularly rich in cultural and artistic diversity.

Along with Veracruz, they are also home to the majority of the population in Mexico who self-identify as Afro-Mexican. In October 2018, in the framework of the 169th Period of Hearings of the Inter-American Commission on Human Rights (IACHR), Veracruz, Oaxaca and Guerrero recognized for the first time the rights of "Afrodescendants" following a petition by civil organizations. On 1 August 2019, after over four centuries of marginalization and exclusion, the Human Rights Commission of the City of Mexico celebrated the constitutional recognition of Afro-Mexican people, villages, and communities by the federal legislative branch, through an addition to Section C, Article 2 of the Political Constitution of the United Mexican States. However, the struggle continues, since Afro-Mexican communities, often also hybridized with Indigenous heritage, are still marginalized, underrepresented, and excluded in Mexico. The Festival emerges then as an artivist (both activist and artistic) response to this local and national context.

Paul Gilroy, a major theorist of the Black Atlantic, considers the crisscrossing movements of Africans across the Atlantic as journeys in which the re-examination of complexities of nationality, location, identity, and historical memory are possible (Gilroy 1993, 16). Building on the emblematic work of W. E. B. Du Bois (1994 [1903]), he maintains that "striving to be both European and black requires some specific forms of double consciousness" (Gilroy 1993, 1). That is, it requires a "sense of always looking at one's self through the eyes of others, of measuring ones's soul by the tape of a world that looks on in amused contempt and pity" (Du Bois 1994[1903], 2). Building on Du Bois' and Gilroy's thinking, we propose that striving to be Mexican and African in the North American context, which often involves further mixed identities through contact with Indigenous populations, and the whole array of intersecting forces and realities they must address, requires specific forms of multiple consciousness. Thus, the festival becomes a crucial heuristic device through which Afro-Mexican communities and allies celebrate the complexities of transnational African identities and heritage in Mexico and their evolution, during and beyond the festival. Its afterlives demonstrate the festival's "poetic and political responsibility toward films, collaborators, programmers, filmmakers, and audiences" (Dramani-Issifou 2023, 265).

It is in this sense that the festival inspires the notion of the Black Pacific, in line with Paul Gilroy's conceptual proposal of the Black Atlantic (Gilroy 1993). Through the curation of a multidisciplinary program of stories about and by Afro-Mexican communities, the festival contributes to "the more ambitious and more useful task of actively reshaping contemporary" Mexico, in this case (Gilroy 1993, 11). And, "in the work of reinterpretation and reconstruction", the festival reinscribes and relocates the African roots of a sector of the Mexican population, thus "creating a new topography" (Gilroy 1993, 16) in which "artistic expression… becomes the means towards both individual self-fashioning and communal liberation" (Gilroy 1993, 40).

The Festival Artístico Audiovisual Afrodescendencias is an anti-racist cultural project which ultimately seeks to foster a dialogue about the current state of cinema, dance and music of African heritage and to understand the role of artistic expressions in the process of liberation, recognition, and struggle in the Afro-Mexican community. The aims of the festival are: (1) to contribute to the visualization of artistic expressions of Indigenous communities of African heritage; (2) to exchange knowledge and experiences with peoples and collectives interested in these cultural expressions of Afro-Mexican identities; and (3) to establish supportive networks between local, national and international academics, artists and activists. It does so through a gender perspective, in that it is mainly led by women and offers a woman-centered program. The festival can thus be understood as a performance of decolonial feminism, in that "it offers a multi-dimensional analysis of oppression and refuses to divide race, sexuality, and class into mutually exclusive categories" (Vergès 2021, 20). It engages with "de-patriarchalizing revolutionary struggles… to assert its *right to existence*" (Vergès 2021, 11). This echoes decolonial thinkers Walter D. Mignolo and Catherine E. Walsh's understanding of nonacceptances as *re-existence*, when they claim: "While not accepting could be termed resistance, our interest and proposition here ... are, more crucially, with *re-existence*, understood as 'the redefining and re-signifying of life in conditions of dignity'" (Mignolo and Walsh 2018, 3).

Although a very recently-established festival, Festival Artístico Audiovisual Afrodescendencias has already created several "afterlives", expanding the ethos beyond the festival dates, thus building year-round sustained audience and community impact, and community dialogues and events. Like the two Canadian case studies, the Festival Artístico Audiovisual Afrodescendencias was forged with local audiences at the forefront of its mission with an itinerant format and spatial decentralization crucial to and coherent with the activist dimension of the festival. The decentralization of festival spaces refers to "an audience-centred curatorial and managerial technique" where the program is spread across multiple locations, reversing the usual or expected direction from people to festival venues (Sendra 2023, 305). Instead, at the Festival Artístico Audiovisual Afrodescendencias, the festival travels to a range of spaces, in collaboration and agreement with them.

In 2024, such spaces included the Museo de Culturas Afromestizas, in Cuajiniculapa, which hosted the engraving exhibition entitled "Afromexicanías: Grabadoras Afrodescendientes", showcasing the work resulting from workshops which ran prior to the festival, led by local artist Ingrid Sáenz, who was also the artist whose design was selected for this festival's edition poster (see Fig. 3). This exhibition provided content to a museum whose visitor numbers had significantly decreased in the past years, and also offered young Afro-Mexican craftswomen a platform to sell their works and continue to grow both their artistic careers and pride in African roots.

During the festival, the guest artist, Tanzanian musician Kyazi Lugangira, based in the United Kingdom, was invited to jam at Mohamed Molina's home, in Cuajiniculapa.[3] The encounter was an opportunity to learn from one another, to share music practices and rhythms, but also, to discuss the ways in which African heritage is present in Mexican music, in instruments such as the "quijada" (an idiophone percussion instrument made from the jawbone of a donkey), the "bote" or "tigrera" (a percussion instrument made from a calabash and a cowhide leather membrane). Community building through creative collaboration resulted in a joint performance on Saturday 8 June, in El Quizá, where the musicians played different songs together, but using styles and stories which

Fig. 3 IV Festival Artístico Audiovisual Afrodescendencias 2024 festival poster (Courtesy Claudia Lora)

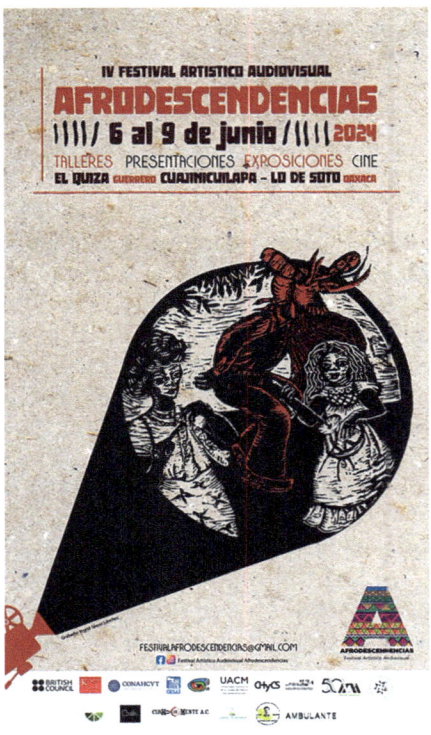

can feed into present and future productions at the festival, and help bolster the musicians' careers.

Workshops further enhanced community building, offering a kind of embodied expression and celebration which were both individual and collective. The festival brought together audiences of different age ranges, from primary school students, children and young teenagers of Afro-Mexican heritage from an orchestra in Lo de Soto, to local (adult) musicians. Serafín Aponte, a graduate of the National Artistic Institute Education of the Fine Arts in Mexico, choreographer, and dance tutor specializing in Afro Dance, delivered dance workshops to local dance tutors and dancers, so that they could continue to teach Afro Dance to additional students, beyond the festival period. One of the dancers who performed on the closing day, as part of the showcase of the workshop results, was Jimena Pastrana, who, during the previous festival (2023), was featured in a short documentary film entitled #*Yo también soy CDMX (#I am also Mexico City)*, directed by Claudia Lora (festival director) and Julián Sacristán (facilitator of the one-minute film workshop). In the film, she reflects on her heritage, as she says: "Now I'm proud to know that my roots come from there [Africa]". She further explains, "It's one of the reasons why one has to sit down and talk about where we come from and the history that wasn't told. It belongs to us Afro-descendants to tell it." The fact that Pastrana is such an active festival participant, or even ambassador, suggests the continuous impact beyond the festival dates.

During the festival, the combination of workshops, facilitators and participants transformed art into a lively and immersive celebration and representation of identity, engaging directly with the community and the location. For instance, both in the printmaking and filmmaking workshop, the global theme was love, either between people, or for Cuajiniculapa. Young audiences were invited to print their productions on T-shirts to take with them, as a souvenir, as an artifact of pride. They also printed it on recycled cardboard, which was exhibited on the closing day of the festival. "I love you, mom" became a leitmotif in the prints, a daughter-mother love, showing awareness of the labor of care, and love by mothers, particularly in an area where migration is a frequent reality.

Similarly, the one-minute films made during the workshops, were all screened on the closing day in the Cuajiniculapa civic square. These also focused on the topic of love, mainly between young teenagers, but also, self-love. Some films were actual love letters to the city of Cuajiniculapa, advocating hope for peace in the region. The topic of love became particularly political, even more so because the films were screened open-air in the evening, in front of the city council of Cuajiniculapa. The screening was followed by a discussion with some of the young people who had made the films, and could now call themselves filmmakers.

Self-representation was the clear festival motto. The evening film program,[4] in the two locations of Cuajiniculapa, was central to the event. It was curated thematically, with a theme per evening, including, "Women, Arts and Knowledge", "Afro-Costeñas Dances in Cinema", "Migration and Diasporas", and "Youth and Diversities". All screenings were preceded by introductions by one of the curators and followed by a discussion with some of the local people involved in the making of the film. On Friday 7 June, the film screened was *Diablos, El Quizá Nueva Generación / Devils, El Quizá New Generation*. The film was the fruits of festival director Claudia Lora's twenty-four years life experience in the region (since 2000). Filmed entirely on location in the area, audiences really enjoyed seeing themselves and beloved ones on screen, with continuous laughter throughout the screening, and words of praise and activist encouragement during the discussion afterward (see Fig. 4).

Screen visibility became an opportunity to learn about the African roots of a large part of the population in the region of Costa Chica, but also, to self-identify, to self-document and to safeguard memories of the rich tangible and intangible cultural heritage of the areas. In 2024, audiences were able to watch African cinema for the very first time. Three Senegalese short films were programmed over the various days: *Dem Dem! / Leaving* (Pape Bouname Lopy, Christophe Rolin, and Marc Recchia, 2017, 24 min.), *La danse des béquilles /The dance of crutches* (Yoro Lidel Niang, 2021, 19 min.) and *Samedi Cinema/ Saturday of Cinema* (Mamadou Dia, 2016, 11 min.).[5] Audiences very much appreciated seeing the African continent as represented by Africans, particularly

Fig. 4 Pop-up screening of *Diablos, El Quizá Nueva Generación* (Claudia Lora, 2024, Mexico) at El Quizá, Guerrero on 7 June 2024 (Courtesy Rodrigo Martínez Vargas)

because the African continent is still very unknown and rather inaccessible for most of the population, despite the strong commitment to fight for the recognition of Afro-Mexican people and the desire to travel to Africa. The Festival Artístico Audiovisual Afrodescendencias is a performance of the Black Pacific, and the artistic showcase and discussions become the seeds to an ongoing liberation struggle and fight for recognition.

5 Concluding Remarks: Funding Challenges and Re-existing in Film Festival Afterlives

The "afterlife" examples we have discussed in this chapter demonstrate that the network of filmmaker-film-spectator is paramount to building communities and social networks off-screen in local communities and throughout the diaspora. This type of network, however, is often dependent on access to resources and there are existing challenges for festivals in building their "lives"—before even developing "afterlives". For example, in 2022 at the AM-FM festival, a discussion was held around sharing resources and building a permanent alliance between Vues d'Afrique, AM-FM and Mostra de Cinemas Africanos in Brazil. The discussion revolved around how AM-FM's original goal was to fashion itself on Vues d'Afrique, who in turn recruits much of its programming from FESPACO. Funding sources vary for each festival and depend on country, region, population, and language. Thus, sharing on a more formal basis becomes complex when, for example, Vues d'Afrique requires French subtitling, AM-FM requires English subtitling and Mostra requires Portuguese subtitling for their various local audiences. Similar challenges exist for the Festival Artístico Audiovisual Afrodescendencias in Costa Chica, where subtitles are done on a volunteer basis by the curators and organizers. Screening and artistic fees for participants are still symbolic, due to limited funding, even for the 2024 edition, when the festival benefited from the British Council program "Circular Culture". With these issues in mind, how is it possible to approach distribution companies for funding as a collective alliance when distribution and exhibition requirements are often regional and national rather than transnational?

The challenges for developing alliances and networks outlined above are monetary. However, the philosophical principle of "giving back" to communities is shared by all the festivals. The art exhibitions, events and filmmaking masterclasses, from the three festivals in Canada and Mexico reinforce the pedagogical responsibility of teaching and learning through story and "giving back" through story. If, in borrowing Reid's (2000) terms festivals, as artworks, are "lives", then the events and workshops with audience-centered discussions, are the "afterlives" that enable the *re-existence* of communities whose cultural heritage is often excluded or invisibilized from official histories. Through the curation of discussion and playful spaces at African film festivals in North America, there is not just a contextualization of films rarely exhibited locally, there is also an opportunity to rethink place, with a kind of topography that is both anti-racist and creative, and which seeks to relocate African roots within the vast populations of Canada, Mexico, and the Black Pacific, more broadly.

Competing Interests Research for this chapter draws on research work developed through Social Sciences and Humanities Research Council of Canada Partnership Development Grant #890–2020-0102.

Notes

1. Due to the COVID-19 global pandemic, the first two editions were hosted in a hybrid format with some activities/workshops across the community and various discussions online.
2. A one-minute video about the festival can be found online at [6 July 2024]: https://www.youtube.com/watch?v=g_bZrRqzHho. Edited by Julián Sacristán, who runs the CINEMINUTO DOCUMENTAL workshops.
3. This participation was made possible by funding from the British Council's 'Circular Culture' program, which the festival secured for the first time in 2024, with Estrella Sendra serving as the required UK-based researcher. The festival has faced financial challenges, since any form of support is ad-hoc, uncertain, and irregular.
4. The fourth edition was co-curated by the director, Claudia Lora, anthropologist and specialist in the dances of the area, mainly the dance known as 'El Diablo' [The Devil], of African heritage, with a masquerade and a very specific mode of clothing; Ana Isabel León, a Mexican researcher on arts and visual culture in Costa Chica; Bianca Pires, a Brazilian researcher based in Mexico, who has also collaborated with Cine Ambulante; Ana Rosa Marques Araujo Teixeira, a Brazilian researcher; and Estrella Sendra, a Spanish researcher based in the United Kingdom with interest in Senegalese cinema

and African film festivals. For the first time, the festival did not just include films from Afro-Mexican regions and communities, but also, from Afro-Brazilian communities, and from Senegal, in the African continent.

5. The program also included a short documentary film by Estrella Sendra on the Festival international de folklore et de percussion in Louga (Senegal).

References

Allen, Chadwick. 2012. A Trans*national* Native American Studies? Why Not Studies that Are Trans-*Indigenous*?. *Journal of Transnational American Studies* 4 (1): 1–22.

Bosma, Peter. 2015. *Film Programming: Curating for Cinemas, Festivals, Archives*. London and New York: Wallflower Press.

Comisión de Derechos Humanos de Ciudad de México. 2019. Reconocimiento Constitucional Federal de las Personas, Pueblos y Comunidades Afromexicanas, Subsana Deuda Histórica Para Su Inclusión. In Boletín Comisión de Derechos Humanos de Ciudad de México 134/2019. Available at 23 July 2024. https://cdhcm.org.mx/2019/08/reconocimiento-constitucional-federal-de-las-personas-pueblos-y-comunidades-afromexicanas-subsana-deuda-historica-para-su-inclusion/#:~:text=1%20de%20agosto%20de%202019&text=La%20adici%C3%B3n%20del%20Apartado%20C,composici%C3%B3n%20pluricultural%20de%20la%20naci%C3%B3n.

Derrida, Jacques. 1996. *Archive Fever: A Freudian Impression*. Chicago: University of Chicago Press.

Dovey, Lindiwe. 2015. *Curating Africa in the Age of Film Festivals*. New York: Palgrave Macmillan.

Dramani-Issifou, Farah Clémentine. 2023. Curating as Care: La Semaine de la Critique and the Marrakech International Film Festival in the Age of Covid-19. In *Rethinking Film Festivals in the Pandemic Era and After*, ed. Marijke de Valck and Antoine Damiens, 255–266. Cham: Palgrave Macmillan.

Du Bois, W. E. B. 1994 [1903]. *The Souls of Black Folk*. New York: Dover Publications.

Gilroy, Paul. 1993. *The Black Atlantic: Modernity and Double Consciousness*. London and New York: Verso.

Glissant, Édouard. 1997. *Traité du Tout-Monde, poétique IV*. Paris: Gallimard.

Glissant, Édouard. 2009. *Philosophie de la Relation*. Paris: Gallimard.

Le Chêne, Gérard, ed. 2024. *Vues d'Afrique 40 ans*. Québec: Bibliothèque et Archives nationales du Québec.

Mignolo, Walter D., and Catherine E. Walsh. 2018. *On Decoloniality: Concepts, Analytics, Praxis*. Durham and London: Duke University Press.

Rastegar, Roya. 2016. Seeing Differently: The Curatorial Potential of Film Festival Programming. In *Film Festivals: History, Theory, Method, Practice*, ed. Marijke de Valck, Brendan Kredell, and Skadi Loist, 181–195. Oxon and New York: Routledge.

Reid, Bill. 2000. *Solitary Raven: the Selected Writings of Bill Reid*. Ed. and intro. Robert Bringhurst. Vancouver: Douglas & McIntyre.

Sendra, Estrella. 2023. Traveling to Audiences: The Decentralization of Festival Spaces at the Festival Films Femmes Afrique in Senegal. *Journal of Festive Studies* 5: 304–325. https://doi.org/10.33823/jfs.2023.5.1.140.

Vergès, Françoise. 2021. *A Decolonial Feminism*. London: Pluto Press.

Wilson, Pamela. 2016. Indigenous Documentary Media. In *Contemporary Documentary*, ed. Daniel Marcus and Selmin Kara, 87–104. London and New York: Routledge.

Open Access This chapter is licensed under the terms of the Creative Commons Attribution 4.0 International License (http://creativecommons.org/licenses/by/4.0/), which permits use, sharing, adaptation, distribution and reproduction in any medium or format, as long as you give appropriate credit to the original author(s) and the source, provide a link to the Creative Commons license and indicate if changes were made.

The images or other third party material in this chapter are included in the chapter's Creative Commons license, unless indicated otherwise in a credit line to the material. If material is not included in the chapter's Creative Commons license and your intended use is not permitted by statutory regulation or exceeds the permitted use, you will need to obtain permission directly from the copyright holder.

Index

A
Aesthetic, 4, 26, 134, 135
Africa
  African cinematic traditions, 135
  African feminism, 43, 51
    negofeminism, 39, 43
  Algeria, 62, 63, 72, 73, 75, 89, 90, 93, 96, 145
  Burkina Faso, 3, 17, 96, 145
    Mossi Empire, 17
  Carthage, 3
  Ghana, 106, 114
  Kenya, 106, 117, 125, 134, 135
  Maghreb, 2, 63, 64, 71
  Morocco, 44, 62, 63, 67, 72, 73, 75, 82, 92–94, 96, 145
  Nigeria, 106, 148
  North Africa, 4, 58, 62, 63, 65, 66, 89, 95
  Pan-African, 6, 16, 18, 105
  Pan-Africanism, 6, 18, 20, 27
  Senegal, 4, 6, 7, 15, 36–47, 49, 51–54, 96, 107, 145, 159
  Tunisia, 3, 73, 75, 94–96, 145
Africa in Motion, 109, 114, 116
African Movie Festival in Manitoba, 4, 9, 124, 128, 136, 144, 146, 150
  Manitoba, 4, 125, 146, 148–150
  Winnipeg, 4, 9, 124, 125, 128, 130, 144, 146–149
Afro-Canadian, 147
Afro-metropolis, 105, 108, 118
Afterlives, 9, 143, 144, 148, 152, 153, 157, 158
  afterlife, 9, 10, 143, 144, 148, 149, 157
  life, lives, 9, 75, 143, 144, 148, 149, 157, 158
Amazigh, 73, 96
  Amazighity, 59, 74
  "Berber", 58, 63, 73
  Imazighen, 62, 71, 73–75, 82
  Tamazgha, 58, 66, 67, 73, 81, 82, 93, 96
Anger management, 125, 133–135
Arab, 15, 59
Archive, 5, 38, 39, 51, 145
  anarchive, 38

living archive, 39, 46
Audience
    abstract audience, 148
    grounded audience, 142, 144, 146, 148
    spectator, 131, 135, 142

B
Black
    Black Atlantic, 151, 152
    Black British, 104–106, 111, 112
    black Caribbean, 105, 107, 111
    Black Pacific, 152, 157, 158
Border, 5, 6, 58, 124, 125
    borderless, 71

C
Cambridge African Film Festival, 116, 117
Centre Yennenga, Dakar, 41, 42, 49
Cinémathèque, 23, 145
City, 5, 8, 22, 45, 48, 65, 69, 92, 102, 104–107, 115, 118, 125, 133, 135, 147–149, 155
City University of New York (CUNY), 59, 65, 67, 87, 88
    LaGuardia Community College, 59, 64, 65, 74, 88
    LaGuardia Performing Arts Center (LPAC), 64, 65, 81, 88, 92, 94
Collaboration, 6, 24, 37, 39–43, 45, 47, 49–51, 68, 88, 116, 118, 129, 153
Community, 6, 7, 9, 59, 65, 71, 81, 84, 86, 88, 92, 95, 111, 114–116, 125, 131, 143, 144, 148, 149, 152–155, 158
Connection, 7, 38, 53, 58, 61, 66–68, 70, 81, 89, 90, 92, 111, 134, 135

Constellations, 6, 7, 37–39, 42, 45, 46, 48, 50–52
COVID-19 pandemic, 71, 73, 80, 87, 132, 133
Creole, 3, 52, 144, 146
Culture
    convergence, 9
    cultural associations, 45
    cultural heritage, 2, 4, 5, 8, 10, 102, 118, 119, 127, 156, 158
        African living cultural heritage, 7, 37
    cultural sovereignty, 2, 143

D
Damiens, Antoine, 8, 36, 38, 79, 80, 85, 90
Decolonization, 3, 59, 106, 108, 109, 119
    decolonize screens, 18
de Valck, Marijke, 8, 36–38, 79, 80, 83–85, 90, 94, 124, 126
Dialogue, 2–5, 8–10, 65, 71, 102, 105, 118, 126, 128, 131, 136, 144–149, 152, 153
Diaspora, 2, 4, 8–10, 15, 18, 20, 24, 36, 40, 52, 66, 69, 71, 74, 96, 102, 104, 109, 110, 112, 118, 119, 124, 136, 144, 157
Diawara, Manthia, 19, 22
Difference, 18, 40, 60, 71, 112, 131
    speak across difference, 65
Diversity, 52, 64–66, 73, 82, 86, 93, 104, 106, 110, 115, 124, 125, 151
Dovey, Lindiwe, 3, 10, 36, 39, 53, 103–106, 108, 109, 111, 113, 116, 118, 119, 142–144, 146, 148
Du Bois, W.E.B., 151

E

Equity, 87, 110
Ethnography, 5, 87
  ethnographic methods, 5
  multi-sited, 38
Exhibition, 2, 36, 73, 102, 103, 109, 114, 118, 130, 144, 146, 147, 153, 157
Expressions, 2, 3, 8, 18, 59, 60, 66, 74, 81, 82, 95, 136, 152, 154
Extractive, 103

F

Facebook, 5, 87, 90
Feminism, 152
FESPACO
  Ouagadougou, 3, 6, 15–17, 19, 21–24, 26, 28, 116
  rituals, 6, 20–23, 72
  Yennenga, Stallion of Yennenga, 6, 17, 23
Festival
  accessibility, 83, 85
  anthropological sites, 58, 61
  awards, 17, 21, 22, 25, 36, 60, 126
  cinephilia, 41
  collaboration, 7, 37, 44, 46, 48, 117, 125, 146, 153
  constellation, 37, 41, 42, 44, 46–48
  curation, 7, 36
  digital platform, 80
  ecosystem, 42, 84, 91
  edition, 46, 72, 107, 146
  experience, 81, 84, 109, 114, 118, 128
  hybrid, 5, 83, 86
  jury, 42, 43, 47, 48, 105, 126
  liveness, 38, 85, 116
  official competition, 21, 24
  online (Zoom), 85, 158
  onsite, 71, 80, 81, 93
  organization, 16, 41, 61, 84, 103, 106, 107
  reciprocity, 45, 47
  streaming, 85
Festival Artistico Audiovisual Afrodescendencias, 4
  Costa Chica, 151, 157
  Mexico, 4
Festival Films Femmes Afrique (FFFA), 4, 7, 37, 39–45, 47, 48, 51
  Dakar, 41, 42
Festival StLouis' DOCS, 7, 39, 45
  Saint-Louis, Senegal, 39, 45, 50
Film
  accessible, 26, 85
  arthouse film, 114
  catalogue, 21, 25, 38, 48, 49, 103, 106, 108–110, 116, 117, 146
  cinema club, 46
  circulation, 6, 36, 38
  competition, 23, 24, 50, 63, 68, 126, 145
  conferences, 23, 61, 63, 144, 146
  co-production, 19, 25, 110, 124
  creative industry, 52
  critics, 19, 21, 26, 36, 43, 46, 49, 85
  curation, 102, 105, 109, 116, 118, 152, 158
  digital, 2, 5, 38, 42, 51, 83, 85–87, 91, 92, 150
  directors, 18, 24, 25, 40, 41, 44, 46–48, 50, 53, 54, 62, 66, 75, 103, 104, 107, 111, 114, 117, 126, 127, 146, 148, 149, 155, 156, 158
  documentary, 17, 39, 40, 42, 45, 46, 49–51, 67–69, 72, 75, 94, 107, 155, 159
  exhibition, 3, 5, 7, 8, 23, 37, 61, 80, 93, 102, 114, 116, 125

traveling exhibition, 130, 132
feature-length, 62
filmmaker, 2, 3, 6–10, 16–20, 23–26, 37, 40–43, 46, 47, 49, 51, 53, 58, 60–63, 66, 67, 69, 71–73, 75, 82, 83, 89, 91–95, 104, 105, 107, 109, 111, 116–118, 124–131, 133–137, 142, 144, 145, 148–150, 152, 155, 157
  auteur, 26, 27
market, 22, 50
masterclass, 51, 149, 150
popular, 22, 27
poster, 23, 46, 145–147, 153
producers, 25, 46, 61–64, 66, 71, 88, 92, 106, 142, 143
production, 3, 7, 19, 37, 49, 53, 59, 62, 64, 71, 73, 90, 110, 129, 145
screenings, 9, 23, 40, 41, 53, 73, 83, 86, 88, 89, 108–111, 114, 115, 125, 127–130, 132, 143, 146, 155, 156
travel, 2, 21, 36, 75, 91, 112, 127, 130, 157
venues, 8, 21, 41, 44, 45, 66, 88, 102, 106, 112, 115, 137, 143, 145, 146, 153
workshops, 155
Film Africa, 4, 8, 102–119
  Brixton, 107, 110, 112, 115
  London, 106–112, 115, 116, 118, 119
Film Festival Research Network, 60
Forum, 8, 10, 81–83, 86–89, 91–94

G

Genre, 8, 49, 72, 81, 93, 96, 119, 125
Gilroy, Paul, 151, 152
Glissant, Edouard, 2, 5, 141–143

Globalization
  global, 2
  local, 2, 125
  national, 124
Guilde africaine des réalisateurs et producteurs, 25

H

Hirak, 96
Home, 64, 69, 70, 75, 83, 88, 89, 105, 147, 151, 153
  homeland, 2, 69

I

Identity
  Afro-Canadian, 4, 136
  Afro-Mexican, 4, 151, 152
  Amazigh, 4, 62–66, 72, 73, 81, 94, 95
Impact, 9, 22, 52, 59, 60, 69, 80, 81, 86, 90, 93–95, 107, 143, 144, 153, 155
Inclusion, 18, 41, 62, 110
Indigenous, 2, 7, 58–62, 65, 66, 69, 71, 73, 74, 81, 82, 84, 87, 95, 127, 143, 147, 148, 151, 152
  Indigenous representational sovereignty, 58, 73
  Native American, 61
Interviews, 22, 81, 87, 90, 91, 95, 117, 119, 133, 134, 146

J

Jallow, Maïmouna, 9, 125, 127–129, 132–137
Journey, 3, 6, 9, 51, 75, 92, 93, 125, 151
  journey of discovery, 5, 7, 59, 71, 73

L

Language, 2, 4, 52, 54, 59, 60, 62, 64, 66–68, 92, 144, 147, 157
Leeds International Film Festival, 4, 40
Leeds, 40
Living Skies Student Film Festival (LSSFF) (Regina, Canada), 128
l'Oeil Vert Collective, 26
Loist, Skadi, 36, 80, 81, 84, 85
London Film Festival, 111, 112

M

Mbembe, Achille, 3, 4, 18
Memory, 4, 20, 69, 73, 89, 90, 94, 151
  collective, 73
Migration, 65, 66, 105, 111, 124, 149, 155
Mostra de Cinemas Africanos, 4, 9, 124, 127, 136, 157
Movement, 3, 6, 25, 26, 70, 73, 94, 96, 107, 144, 151
Multicultural, 8, 102, 125, 129, 131
Multidirectional, 5, 44, 73
Multidisciplinary, 4, 8, 65, 88, 102, 115, 151, 152
Myth, 6, 16, 17, 20, 24, 26, 27

N

Nairobi, 125, 133–135, 137
Neighborhood, 8, 45, 46, 50, 65, 102, 134
New York Forum of Amazigh Film (NYFAF), 4, 7, 8, 57, 59, 61, 63–73, 75, 80–83, 86–95
New York, 64

O

Origin, 4, 19, 20, 45, 51, 74, 105, 119

Ouagadougou, 20

P

Participation, 10, 38, 42, 47, 66, 67, 82, 85, 129, 144, 158
Pedagogical, 4, 7, 8, 65, 67, 71, 73, 82, 83, 148, 157
Peirano, Maria Paz, 38, 46, 49, 60, 61, 71, 83, 84
Philosophy, 5
Place, 3, 5, 8, 9, 16, 20, 21, 28, 38, 40, 42, 46, 50, 59, 61, 63, 66, 67, 69, 70, 72, 81, 84, 85, 88, 92–96, 102, 104, 107, 109, 110, 130, 132–134, 146, 148–150, 158
  location, 5, 7, 8, 22, 51, 58–60, 65, 66, 71, 72
  space, 2–4, 9, 21, 23, 66, 67, 69–71, 73, 82, 85, 87, 90, 148, 153, 158
    decentralization of festival spaces, 153
Positionalities, 103, 118
Post-colonial, 69
Process, 4, 5, 10, 48, 59, 61, 63, 66, 67, 73, 85, 103, 107–110, 117, 128, 129, 143, 144, 148, 152
Program, 15, 18, 38, 40, 46, 65, 67–69, 72, 82, 84, 85, 87, 88, 92–94, 110, 111, 115, 117, 126, 128, 130, 131, 142, 144–146, 150, 152, 153, 155, 157–159
  programming intervention, 131

R

Rallye-Expos, 146, 147
Relational, 5, 7, 59, 109, 110, 143
  relationality, 110
Representation
  misrepresentation, 40, 108

sovereignty, 7
under-representation, 41, 108
Research, 2, 10, 37, 38, 52, 53, 60, 62, 73, 96, 103, 118, 119, 127, 128, 137, 142
  field, 9, 60, 102
Royal African Society (RAS), 104, 106, 107, 117, 119

S
Sankara, Thomas, 18–20
Sembène, Ousmane, 6, 13, 15, 16, 20, 22, 25, 145
Sustainability, 6, 41, 64, 68, 83, 117, 131

T
TANO, 116–118
Television, 16, 19, 22, 27, 49, 82, 106
Theater, 80, 86, 88–90, 132
Transgenerational, 88
Translation, 60, 82, 128
  intercultural, 67
Translocality, 69, 70
Transnational, 2–5, 8, 9, 18, 51, 66, 67, 71, 74, 82, 83, 85, 92, 94, 124, 125, 128–131, 135–137, 143, 145, 148, 152, 157
  transnational flow, 4, 7, 37, 118, 127, 129, 131, 133, 135, 136

Travelling, 2

U
United Kingdom
  England, 104, 106
  Scotland, 109
  Wales, 104, 116
United Nations, 109, 149

V
Video, 26, 27, 53, 58, 62, 63, 70, 75, 114, 133, 158
  Zoom videos, 134
Vieyra, Paulin Soumanou, 15, 21
Virtualization, 8, 95
Visualization, 47, 48, 51, 152
  mind-mapping, 38
Vues d'Afrique, 3, 5, 9, 23, 86, 124–128, 130, 136, 144–147, 157
  Montreal, 9, 23, 124, 129, 144, 145
  Québec, 9

W
Watch-Africa (Wales), 116, 117
Windrush, 105
Women, 23, 24, 39–44, 50, 51, 72, 75, 90, 92, 94, 96, 152, 155
  African women, 23, 24, 40, 129

GPSR Compliance

The European Union's (EU) General Product Safety Regulation (GPSR) is a set of rules that requires consumer products to be safe and our obligations to ensure this.

If you have any concerns about our products, you can contact us on ProductSafety@springernature.com

In case Publisher is established outside the EU, the EU authorized representative is:

Springer Nature Customer Service Center GmbH
Europaplatz 3
69115 Heidelberg, Germany

Batch number: 08604708

Printed by Printforce, the Netherlands